D1175386

RENAISSANCE STUDIES

RENAISSANCE STUDIES

Six Essays

EDITED BY

I. D. McFARLANE

A. H. ASHE   D. D. R. OWEN

Rowman and Littlefield

Totowa, New Jersey 07512

1972

Library • St. Joseph's College
222 Clinton Avenue
Brooklyn, N. Y. 11205

Reprinted from
FORUM FOR MODERN LANGUAGE STUDIES
Volume VIII No. 4

———

First published in the United States 1972
by *Rowun and Littlefield, Totowa, New Jersey*
ISBN 0-87471-106-1

©Forum for Modern Language Studies 1971

All rights reserved. No part of this publication may be reproduced, stored in a retrieval system, or transmitted, in any
form, or by any means, electronic, mechanical, photocopying,
recording or otherwise, without the prior permission of the
Scottish Academic Press Ltd., 25 Perth Street, Edinburgh.
EH3 5DW

Printed in Great Britain by
W. C. Henderson & Son Ltd., St. Andrews

FOREWORD

The scholars who have contributed to this volume share a common purpose : to present new ideas and information on some aspect of Renaissance literature. The editorial hand has been light. No attempt has been made to ensure conformity of method, still less to impose an overall plan or seek some artificial unity or illusion of comprehensiveness. The result is a collection of independent studies, whose interest lies in two directions : neo-Latin writings and the poetry of the Pléiade and its satellites.

J. IJsewijn draws attention to the need for more texts of neo-Latin authors to be properly edited. He gives a model illustration of his view by his edition of a hitherto unpublished composition of Alexander Hegius which throws light on the issues involved in the growing conflict between medieval philosophical methods and the new philology. I. D. McFarlane offers a preliminary history of George Buchanan's Psalm paraphrases : here much more research needs to be done on the genesis of these paraphrases, both in the matter of the humanist's motivation and of the sources, classical and exegetical, on which he must have drawn. We also need to know more about the relations of the various editions published during Buchanan's lifetime, and indeed on those published later ; and there is something more to be learned about the reception of the paraphrases in Europe : a Polish colleague has noted their impact in his country, and further enquiry into their fortunes in eastern Europe would be worthwhile.

The articles centering on the Pléiade are symptomatic of the new perspectives in which sixteenth-century French poetry is now being studied. Grahame Castor explores the theme of illusion in Ronsard. This is a key theme in the understanding of the poet, and here it is studied in the later love-poetry, the *Sonets pour Helene*, and in the variants Ronsard introduced into the *Amours* written when he was just embarked on his career. Malcolm Quainton concerns himself with problems of sources in Jean-Antoine de Baïf, who has remained in the penumbra of research until fairly recently. It is certainly time for the poet to be looked at in a new light since the publication, many decades ago, of Augé-Chiquet's biography. C. N. Smith offers us a reassessment of Jacques de la Taille's tragedies : little work has been done on this author since Dabney's monograph (1934) until quite recently ; and with the current reappraisal of Neoclassical tragedy in Renaissance France this study comes at an opportune moment. Finally, Peter Sharratt gives a bibliographical *bonne bouche*, a note on the discovery of an unknown Amyot edition.

101254

CONTRIBUTORS

J. IJSEWIJN is Professor and Director of the Seminarium Philologiae Humanisticae, University of Louvain. Editor of *Humanistica Lovaniensia*, he is in the forefront of the revival of neo-Latin studies.

I. D. McFARLANE, until recently Buchanan Professor of French Language and Literature at the University of St Andrews, is now at Oxford. He is the author of an edition of Scève's *Délie* and of articles on neo-Latin poets.

GRAHAME CASTOR, sometime Fellow and Senior Tutor of Gonville and Caius College, Cambridge, is now teaching at the University of Warwick. Author of *Pléiade Poetics* (1964), he is at present working on Ronsard.

MALCOLM QUAINTON is a Lecturer in the University of Lancaster and author of several articles on Ronsard and of an anthology of Baïf's poems (1970).

C. N. SMITH, formerly a Lecturer at Aberdeen, is now teaching at the University of East Anglia. His doctoral thesis was on the La Taille brothers ; he has completed an edition of the tragedies by Montchrestien and is at present working on the French emblematists.

PETER SHARRATT is a Lecturer in the University of Edinburgh and author of a doctoral thesis on Pierre de la Ramée's literary ideas. He has published a number of articles on sixteenth-century and contemporary authors.

CONTENTS

I

ALEXANDER HEGIUS (+ 1498)
INVECTIVA IN MODOS SIGNIFICANDI

Text, Introduction and Notes

I. Introduction

One of the first and foremost tasks the neo-Latin scholar has to do now is to make trustworthy editions of as many works as possible of humanistic authors, which we still must read in manuscript or early printings. As a matter of fact our modern means of reproduction of original documents such as microfilm, xerocopy or even anastatic reprint, do not at all diminish the urgent need of new editions. In the first place, our abuse nowadays of photographical reproduction combined with a generalised frequent consultation of the originals will destroy in a short time, or, at least, damage seriously manuscripts and incunabula, which were not made for such " ill-treatment ". Apart from that, many scholars interested in the history of literature, philosophy, education or sciences are not and need not be trained specialists in palaeographical problems. Finally, it always takes much more time to make one's way through 15th or 16th century books than to read them in a modern edition : anomalous punctuation, bad printing types, unclear hands, abbreviations and errors of all kind continuously hinder the scholar in his work, whereas unidentified names and quotations or the absence of indexes take up much of the time of many readers. Can we imagine what would be the present state of classical studies if there were not the great critical collections of Greek and Roman texts ? The neo-Latin scholar now often works in conditions most comparable to those in which early humanists toiled at classical authors.

The purpose of this study is to publish for the first time since 1503 a short but important polemical work by Alexander Hegius (ca. 1433-1498), that famous Westphalian schoolmaster,[1] who was the first, so it seems, to introduce some humanistic ideas into the teaching of Latin at St-Lebuin's school at Deventer : " *Ea schola tunc adhuc erat barbara . . . nisi quod Alexander Hegius et Zinthius coeperant aliquid melioris litteraturae invehere* ", so we read in the *Compendium vitae Erasmi*.[2]

Modern appreciations of Hegius' work are conflicting : Lindeboom declared himself disappointed by the reading of his treatises—yet he singles out the invective as the most important—and asked how the Westphalian schoolmaster ever got such a famous reputation.[3] But recently Professor H. O. Burger called him the third great schoolman of his century, the two other ones being the Italian Vittorino da Feltre and Guarino da Verona.[4]

Be it as this may, one cannot deny the fact that Hegius plays a quite considerable part in the beginnings of humanistic Latin teaching and literature in the Northern Low Countries.

Hegius' collected works in both prose and poetry were posthumously published at Deventer by Jacobus Faber in two volumes.[5] The first one bears the following title :

Alexandri Hegii Gymnasi | archę iampridem Daventriensis diligentissimi ar | tium professoris clarissimi philosophi presbyteri | poetę utriusque linguę docti Carmina et gracia et | elegantia ; cum ceteris eius opusculis quę subiciuntur—
De scientia et eo quod scitur contra Academicos |
De triplici anima vegetabili : sensili : et rationali |
De vera pasche inveniendi ratione Quam ex Isaac |
Argyro greco excepisse apparet De Rhetorica De |
arte et inertia |
De sensu et sensili De moribus |
De philosophia |
De incarnationis misterio Erotemata.

This title is misleading as the volume contains only the *Carmina* and not the *cetera opuscula*. The pages are numbered from Aii to Eiiii. At the end (p. 63 in modern numbering) one reads the colophon :

Impressum Daventrie per me Richardum
paffraet Anno Dñi. M.CCCCC.iii. Mensis
Julii. vicesimo nono

[1] J. Lindeboom, *Het bijbelsch humanisme in Nederland*, Leiden, 1913 ; P. N. M. Bot, *Humanisme en Onderwijs in Nederland*, Utrecht, 1955 ; J. Esterhues, art. *Hegius*, in : *Lexikon f. Theologie und Kirche*, V (1960²), p. 61.

[2] Cf. P. S. Allen, *Opus Epistolarum D. Erasmi*, I, p. 48, ll. 34-37.

[3] Op. laud. (note 1), pp. 70-81, with an analysis of the works. Hegius' reputation is very old. A Flemish grammarian, Livinus Crucius, in his *Collectanea in Syntaxim Badianam ex optimis quibusque authoribus* (1521) writes on the first page of his preface : *Nam si disertissimo oratori, poetae ac philosopho Alexandro Hegio placet. . . .*

[4] H. O. Burger, *Renaissance-Humanismus - Reformation. Deutsche Literatur im Europäischen Kontext*, Bad Homburg, 1969, p. 120.

[5] For this study and edition we made use of the copy preserved in the Royal Library at The Hague (The Netherlands).

Faber's edition certainly does not contain the whole output of Hegius' poetical writings. A manuscript at Prague—Ms. 44. G. 79—preserves three poems by Hegius, one of them not to be found in the Deventer edition.[6] It is a *Hymnus post cibum* (ff. 61ᵛ-63ᵛ) beginning with the verse :
Pastis visceribus ciboque sumpto.

The second and much more voluminous part (pages running from Aii to Oiii or 170 in total) bears this title :

Alexandri Hegii artium ma | gistri Gymnasiarche quondam Daven-
triensis phi | losophi presbyteri utriusque linguę docti Dialogi. |
—De scientia et eo quod scitur contra Academicos.
—De tribus animę generibus.
—De incarnationis misterio Dialogi quo Quibus | additum de paschę et
celebratione et inventione.
—Dialogus physicus
—De sensu et sensili
—De arte et inertia
—De Rhetorica
—De moribus
—Eiusdem Farrago Cui addita Invectiva eius in | modos significandi
quos refellit verissime
—Epistola una et altera eius ceteris apud | suos latentibus.

The colophon of this part reads as follows :
Impressum Daventrię Per me Richardum | pafraet. Anno dñi.
M.CCCCC.iii. In profesto Circumcisionis dñi.

Some of these prose works (*De arte et inertia* ; *Farrago*) survive also in earlier separate editions. Only the letters and a choice of poems have been re-edited by modern scholars.[7]

For the history of humanistic or Renaissance Latin the *invectiva in modos significandi* is by far the most important of the prose works. Its contents can be divided into two parts of rather unequal length.

The first one (§§ 1-30 in our edition) is the invective proper, in which the humanistic thesis is proposed in an often violent tone. This thesis says that a *grammaticus* is a teacher, who knows the correct use of the language —be it Latin or Dutch—, not he who makes all kind of philosophical reflections on linguistic terminology most of the time in a barbarous wording. As an example of such disreputable philosophers of language or *modistae* Hegius cites the name of Michael of Marbaix.

In these pages Hegius follows in the track of the Italian humanists, whose influence was penetrating more and more to the North of Europe. A similar attack against the mediaeval philosophers of language can be read e.g. in Valla's speech in praise of Thomas Aquinas :

Ista autem, quae vocant metaphysica et modos significandi et alia id
genus, quae recentes theologi tamquam novam sphaeram nuper inventam

---

[6] Cf. J. Truhlar, *Catalogus codicum mss. Latinorum qui in C. R. bibliotheca publica atque universitatis Pragensis asservantur*, Prague 1905-1906, *1331*. A microfilm copy of the pages 60ᵛ-63ᵛand 65ᵛ-66ʳ is kept at Louvain in the Seminarium Philologiae Humanisticae of the University.

[7] Cf. J. Lindeboom, op. laud. (note 1), p. 72, n.2.

aut planetarum epicyclos admirantur, nequaquam ego tantopere admiror nec ita multum interesse arbitror scias an nescias, et quae forte sit satius nescire tamquam meliorum impedimenta.[8]
Hegius' invective against the *modi* was more than a mere literary exercise. It was a most timely plea for a better education, adapted to the needs and the minds of children. To realize that we should remember what Erasmus tells us of his own bitter and hard experiences at school :

> *Sed infelicior erat aetas, quae me puero modis significandi et quaestiunculis ex qua vi pueros excarnificabat nec aliud interim docens quam perperam loqui.*[9]

The lecture of Hegius' invective perhaps resuscitated in Erasmus his aversion from the " modistae " about 1500. In fact, in the second version of his *Antibarbari*, published 1520, he added a violent attack against the *insulsissimus auctor* Michael modista, which is not to be found in the original draft, written at Halsteren in 1494-95.[10]

Moreover, the *modi significandi* were a paedagogical problem all over Europe. We quoted already the Italian Valla. Let us recall also chapter XIV of Rabelais' *Gargantua*, who still in the second quarter of the 16th century includes a *De modis significandi* among the Latin books studied by Gargantua. In 1500 Timannus Kemenerus, school-director at Münster/Westphalia, published an *Epistola in regiminum vires modosque significandi*, which we print as an appendix to the present study.[11] A Polish *De modis significandi* of the same years will be discussed below. [Cf. also P. S., p. 318.]

The second part of Hegius' invective (our §§ 31-40) broadens its subject into a general condemnation of all bad schoolbooks, particularly barbarous dictionaries of the late Middle Ages, i.e. of Hegius' own time.

The first book he proposes to expel from the school is the treatise *De Scholarium Disciplina* of pseudo-Boethius, which was very popular at that time.[12] Arnold Geilhoven of Rotterdam (13. .-1442) says of it in his *Somnium Doctrinale* : *Debitus autem et rectus ordo proficiendi in sciencia est ille quem docet Boecius, De Disciplina Scolarium . . .,*[13] the same thing also which once Quintilian has said about Cicero. It was edited i.a. at Louvain in 1485, at Deventer in 1490, 1496, 1500 etc.[14] After Hegius the German humanist Henricus Bebel (1472-1518) attacked it in his discourse *Qui auc-*

---

[8] This *Encomium* has been edited for the first time by J. Vahlen in the *Vierteljahrschrift für Kultur und Literatur der Renaissance*, 1 (1886), pp. 384-396. See the passage quoted p. 394. Vahlen's edition is reprinted in *Laurentius Valla, Opera omnia*, con una premessa di E. Garin, Torino 1962, vol. II, pp. 339-352. See p. 350.

[9] *De pueris statim ac liberaliter instituendis*, ed. J. Margolin, Genève 1966, p. 461 = LB I, 514E=Erasmi Opera Omnia I, 2, Amsterdam 1971, p. 77.

[10] Erasmi *Opera omnia*, I 1, Amsterdam 1969, p. 58, ll. 10-11 ; p. 61, l. 16.

[11] On Timannus Kemenerus see our note to § 39 of the text edition below.

[12] See notes 13-15 and our commentary to § 31 of the text below.

[13] The text is quoted from the unedited Amsterdam manuscript by N. Mann, *Arnold Geilhoven : an Early Disciple of Petrarch in the Low Countries*, in : *Journal of the Warburg and Courtauld Institutes*, XXXII (1969), pp. 73-108. See p. 87.

[14] See i.a. the *Short-title Catalogue of Books printed in the Netherlands and Belgium . . . from 1470 to 1600 now in the British Museum*, London 1965, p. 37.

tores legendi sint novitiis ad comparandam eloquentiam et qui fugiendi (Pforz-
heim 1504), where he says : *Caeteros autem versificatores* (i.e. the mediaeval
poets, to be distinguished from the ancient and humanistic *poetae*) . . .,
*item . . . Boecium De Disciplina Scholarium . . . tamquam pestiferos decli-
nabis.* . . .[15]

The very queer Latin of this *Disciplina* brings Hegius to the common
humanist thesis that we should use the Latin words in the sense the old
authors did. Hegius speaks here much in the same way as the greater
Italian humanists, i.a. Valla. But in his views he is not a narrow-minded
Ciceronian, not an Erasmian *Nosoponus*, since he never limited the ancient
writers to Cicero alone, but included also many christian authors and even
Bernardus.[16]

From this thesis Hegius quite logically draws the conclusion that the
use of barbarous mediaeval vocabularies and dictionaries should be abolished
in the class-room and that their place should be taken by ancient sources
as Varro, Festus and Nonius, or humanistic ones as Tortelli.

Hegius' categorical rejection of bad vocabularies is not a new phenomenon in Latin literature. It may be rather paradoxical to see that some
of these books were condemned sweepingly by mediaeval scholars but still
freely used by men commonly called humanists. Roger Bacon (1214-1292)
in his *Compendium studii philosophiae* calls Papias, Hugutio and Brito *men-
daces, quorum mendaciis vulgus opprimitur Latinorum*.[17] Yet Petrarch uses
Hugutio[18] and the Florentine chancellor Coluccio Salutati (1331-1406) draws
heavily from both Papias and Hugutio in his *De laboribus Herculis*, a work
of mature age. On the other hand, John of Garland (ca. 1195-ca. 1275),
whose Latin style hardly can be qualified as elegant and who was treated
himself with much disdain by Erasmus and other humanists, speaks very
scornfully of Ebrardus of Béthune in chapter XIV of his *Morale Scholarium*,[19]
v. 359 sqq. : *Mendax Grecismus est.* . . .

The end of Hegius' invective causes serious critical trouble : as it stands,
paragraph 39 of our edition cannot be written by Hegius because it mentions
at least one work published just two years after his death. This is the reason

---

[15] We owe this reference to : *Quinque Claves Sapientiae, recensuit* A. Vidmanovà-
Schmidtovà, Leipzig, Bibliotheca Teubneriana 1970, pp. XXXV-XXXVI, who took it
from a study by R. Avesani.

[16] See § 28 of the text. Bernardus *melleus ore* is also cited as an authority together
with Cicero, Horace, Ambrose, Augustine and even Peter of Blois in the *De arte dic-
tandi* of Engelbert Schut of Leiden (written 1454 ; printed at Gouda, probably in 1480 ;
the text also in J. Noels, *Leven en Werk van Engelbert Schut,* unpubl. dissert., Louvain
1970).

[17] We owe this quotation to J. J. Baebler, *Beiträge zu einer Geschichte der lateinischen
Grammatik im Mittelalter,* Halle a.S. 1885, pp. 69-70.

[18] Elisabeth Pellegrin, *Un manuscrit des " Derivationes " d'Osbern de Gloucester
annoté par Pétrarque,* in : *Italia Medioevale e Umanistica,* III (1960), pp. 263-266.

[19] L. J. Paetow, *Morale Scolarium of John of Garland (Johannes de Garlandia),
Edited with an Introduction . . .,* Berkeley-California 1927, p. 223. In the same chapter
Garland condemns also the *Doctrinale of Alexander de Villa Dei,* which remained in
general use, at least outside Italy, till after 1500 !

6

why we put this paragraph between square brackets. Possibly other paragraphs also were added to the text of the invective after the death of Hegius, perhaps by his editor James Faber of Deventer. There are no means, however, to distinguish them from the genuine ones.

Before proceeding to textual and editorial problems we should like to say some words concerning the historical meaning of Hegius' attack on the *modi significandi* apart from the paedagogical one discussed above.

In his study on the evolution of linguistic theory during the Middle Ages the Danish scholar J. Pinborg[20] has pointed out that the humanistic hostility against the *modi* is quite different from the philosophical opposition to them by late 14th and 15th century nominalists such as Pierre d'Ailly and others. Pinborg quotes also a very interesting text from a treatise *De modis significandi* by a younger Polish contemporary of Hegius, viz. John Stobniczy from Krakow (1470-1518), who—strangely enough—appears to be a kind of humanist and scotist at the same time. Stobniczy fully recognizes the importance of studying good Latin authors : . . . *licet magis probem horum sententiam, qui artem grammatice, hoc est recte loquendi scientiam, addiscunt sepe relegendo libros poetarum, oratorum, historicorum ac aliorum . . .*, but nevertheless he thinks that the *modi significandi* can be useful in some respect : *non tamen omnino contemnendam esse considerationem modorum significandi censeo, quippe quod pleraque ad cognitionem partium orationis earumque accidentium pertinentia ex consideratione modorum significandi facilius sciri possunt. . . .*

This conciliatory thesis obviously met with little or no success among the humanists, whose main concern was the restoration of the " better " Latin in education and literature and who did not care for the speculations of abstract mediaeval philosophy, often considered as a symbol of " gothic barbarism ". Therefore we don't believe, as does Pinborg, that the humanistic point of view would not have prevailed if its way had not been prepared by the nominalist undermining of the philosophical basis of the *modi*. In fact, the world of humanism on one side and that of mediaeval philosophy on the other in general are so sharply separated that the *modi* did not have any chance to survive in humanistic schools, even if philosophers remained attached to them for several generations more. Valla did not need the treatise of Pierre d'Ailly, nor did Hegius, to come to their opinion concerning the *modi* or to proceed to a fundamental reformation of the Latin grammar school.

★   ★   ★

The history of the text of Hegius' invective presents two stages. As far as we could ascertain the complete text is to be found only in the 1503 edition of the *Dialogi*, where it concludes the volume except for two letters which follow it. Further on we designate it as edition D.

[20] J. Pinborg, *Die Entwicklung der Sprachtheorie im Mittelalter*, Münster-W. 1967, pp. 210-211.

Paragraphs 1-10 of our edition were printed much earlier but not as an independent work. These paragraphs as well as the title *Contra eos qui modorum*, etc. were incorporated in a collection of notes on Latin grammar, published many times under the title *Farrago*. This *Farrago* precedes the invective in the *Dialogi*, but of course without the passage *Contra eos*, etc.

Here is a list of the known editions of the *Farrago*, compiled on the basis of Campbell, *Annales de la typographie néerlandaise au XVᵉ siècle*, its two supplements by M. E. Kronenberg, and W. Nijhoff-M. E. Kronenberg, *Nederlandsche Bibliographie van 1500 tot 1540*. We designate these editions by the marks Fa, Fb, Fc, etc.

—Fa : [Deventer, Richard Paffraet, about 1480]. Campbell (= Kronenberg, *More Contributions*) 909bb.
—Fb : [Deventer, Jacobus de Breda, about 1486]. Campbell 738.
—Fc : [Deventer, Jacobus de Breda, about 1487]. Campbell 739.
—Fd : [Deventer, Richard Paffraet], 30 Sept. 1490. Campbell 740.
—Fe : [Deventer, Richard Paffraet, ca. 1490]. Campbell 741.
—Ff : Deventer, [Richard Paffraet], 14 July 1495. Campbell 742.
—Fg : Deventer, [Jacobus de Breda], 7 August 1496. Campbell 743.
—Fh : Deventer, [Jacobus de Breda], 18 Oct. 1498. Campbell (= Kronenberg, *Contribution*), 909c.
—Fi : [Deventer, Richard or Albert Paffraet, 1498 or after 1500 ?]. Campbell (= Kronenberg, *Contribution*), 909d = W. Nijhoff-M. E. Kronenberg, vol. II, nr. 3143.
—Fj : Deventer, [Jacobus de Breda], 28 July 1502. Nijhoff-Kronenberg, vol. I, nr. 1044.

Most of these editions survive in only one copy. We have seen personally Fa, Fb and Ff at the Royal Library of The Hague, and Fe at the Royal Library of Brussels. Moreover, Dr R. Engelberts checked for us Fd and Fj at the University Library of Utrecht. From this it is clear that edition Ff introduced some corruptions in the text, which were to remain through all the succeeding printings and even in the *Dialogi* : so *Ex quo liquet* in § 4 became *Et quamlibet modorum*, which makes no sense, whereas in § 6 *perficere* was changed erroneously into *proficere*.

The text of paragraphs 1-10 in the *Farrago* was intercalated between the notices on *congruitas* and *ambiguitas*. It followed, often without any distinctive mark, immediately after : . . . *quoniam Ick pronomen teutonicum primae personae non congruit verbo* bist *secundae personae*. Again without any transition the end of § 10 (*quot aureorum tuus*) is followed by reflections on the polysemantic nouns : *Habemus ambiguas orationes, ambiguas partes orationis*. . . So the first draft of the invective has nothing of an independent work, and only after the *Dialogi* came out, could it be considered as such. This was already done by an unknown 16th century reader of Fd, who wrote, in margin, *de modis significandi* at the beginning of the text and put a mark / at the end.

In the apparatus criticus of our edition we noted all the important divergences of Fa, Fb, Fe, Ff and D, but passed over in silence obvious misprints without consequence (e.g. *sad* for *sed*). We noted also the corrections we were obliged to make in the paragraphs 11-40, for which D is the only but not always reliable testimony.

Since there is no consistence at all in the spelling of *ae* (one finds *e* as well as *ę* as well as *ae*) we always put *ae* in flexional endings, including pronouns as *haec*. In all other cases it was possible to respect the old editions. We are well aware of the fact that, so doing, we use an orthography which is hardly less queer than that of Paffraet and Jacobus de Breda. Perhaps it was more " fifteenth-century " to write always *e* instead of *ae*, but we gave some weight to the modern reader's convenience.[21]

II. Text

Contra modos significandi Invectiva Alexandri Hegii

Contra eos qui modorum significandi noticiam credunt grammatico necessariam, qui novo nomine modistae vocantur.

1   1. Qui dicunt modorum significandi noticiam efficere grammaticum falluntur. Non propterea quispiam grammaticus dicitur, quia scit modum significandi materialem nominis eum esse, qui nomini cum pronomine communis est et formalem, eum, qui nomini proprius est ;
5 sed qui scit latine loqui et scribere, is grammatici nomine dignus est.

  2. Nemo negatur propterea esse grammaticus, quod nescit qui sint modi significandi essentiales et accidentales, materiales et formales, absoluti et respectivi partium orationis ; sed qui recte loqui et scribere nescit, quantumcumque verborum de modis significandi faciat, gram-
10 matici nomine indignus est.

  3. Non is dicitur grammaticus, qui scit genitivum casum significare per modum *ut cuius est alterum*, sed qui scit non recte dici *genitivum significare per modum ut cuius est alterum*.

  4. Grammatici qui de modis significandi scripserunt, si quidem
15 grammatici dicendi sunt, barbare scripserunt. Veteres autem, qui ne verbum quidem de eis fecere, rectissime locuti sunt. Ex quo liquet modorum significandi noticiam non solum non prodesse, sed vehementer officere eis qui grammaticam profitentur. Cur Itali non docent pueros modos significandi nisi quia eos cariores habent quam ut eis tam
20 inutilia tamque noxia inculcent ?

  5. Quid prodest scire quod modus significandi materialis pronominis est significare per modum *habitus et quietis*, formalis autem per modum *determinatae apprehensionis*, si nescias latinius dici : *liber est meus* quam *liber est mei* ; *liber est meus ipsius* quam *liber est mei ipsius* ; *liber est*

[21] We should like to thank here Dr C. Reedijk, chief librarian of the Royal Library at The Hague, and Dr R. Engelberts, Institute of Classical Studies of the University of Utrecht, for the promptness and the kindness of their help at this work.

25 *meus et Joannis* quam *liber est mei et Joannis* ; *liber est meus qui lego*
quam *liber est mei qui lego* ?

    6. Quid prodest noticia modorum significandi, si nescias has ora-
tiones esse barbaras et viciosas : *Ego dedi sibi librum* ; *tu dedisti sibi
librum. Ego misereor sui* ; *tu misereris sui. Ego diligo socium suum* ;
30 *tu diligis socium suum.*

    Pueris danda est opera ut sciant quae constructio debeatur prono-
minibus relativis reciprocis, quae non reciprocis ; hoc est : ut sciant
quando utendum sit pronomine *suus,* quando pronomine *is* aut *eius*
obliquis. *Joannes diligit socium suum* recte dicitur. Pronomen enim
35 *suus* tunc recte apponitur verbo, cum antecedens eius verbo supponitur.
Ut : *Joannes socium suum diligit.*

    Qui pronomen reciprocum pro non reciproco ponit, non recte loqui-
tur. Itemque qui non reciprocum pro reciproco ponit a viciis liber non
est. *Joannes socium suum diligit* oratio perfecta est. *Joannes diligit*
40 *socium eius* oratio imperfecta est, quam sic poterimus perficere :
Joannes diligit socium eius, cui heri librum commodavi.

    7. Modi significandi non efficiunt constructionem partium orationis.
Genitivus enim *mei* habet eum modum significandi, quem ceteri
genitivi, et non habet constructionem ceterorum genitivorum. Recte
45 enim dicitur : *liber Joannis,* sed non recte dicitur *liber mei.* Recte
dicitur *liber est Joannis,* non recte *liber est mei.*

    8. Quid prodest genitivo *mei* significare *rem cuius est alterum,* cum
non possit construi cum nomine significante rem, quae alterius est,
siquidem *liber mei* non recte dicitur.

50   9. *Que* coniunctio habet modum significandi, quem *et* coniunctio ;
et non habet constructionem, quam *et* coniunctio. Recte enim dicitur
Ego et tu damus, non recte autem *Ego que tu damus.*

    10. *An* et *ne* eundem modum significandi habent, sed non eandem
constructionem. Recte enim dicitur : *An Joannes est domi ?* non recte
55 *ne Joannes est domi ?*

    Tenus et *versus* prepositiones eum modum significandi habent,
quem ceterae prepositiones, sed non eandem constructionem quam
ceterae. Recte enim dicitur *in capulo,* non recte *tenus capulo.* Dicendum
enim *capulo tenus.* Cui modo significandi debent hi genitivi *pluris*
60 *minoris tanti quanti,* quod construuntur cum verbis ad emendum et
vendendum pertinentibus, potius quam hi genitivi *aureorum philip-
porum,* hoc est cur latine dicitur : *Liber meus tanti emptus est, quanti
tuus,* cum non dicatur latine : *liber meus tot aureorum emptus est, quot
aureorum tuus ?*

65   11. Si Grammatica, quae ars loquendi est, ipsa loqui posset, non
dubium, quin incandesceret vehementer in eos, qui eam ita excarnificant, ita fedant ut ne grammatica quidem dici digna sit. Grammatica
certe ars liberalis est. Non omnes autem, sed ea Grammatica quae est
ars et recte loquendi et scribendi. Illa autem quae nunc a pueris

70   magna mercede discitur, vix ars liberalis vocanda est, quoniam non
recte sed barbare loquendi ars est. Itaque indigna est haec, quam nunc
pueri plerique a preceptoribus suis discunt, quae ars liberalis dicatur,
non illa autem, quae recte et loquendi et scribendi ars. Corrumpuntur
enim nunc nomina librorum, nunc artium, nunc figurarum, nunc
75   vocabula a Graecis commodate accepta. Adeo exigua latinitatis cura
est ut etiam titulo librorum corrumpantur ! Teutonica lingua plus
ideotis debet, quam latina lingua litteratis. Illi enim operam dant ut
recte loquantur et non corrumpant linguam suam. Hi vero nequ die
agunt ut recte loquantur, neque turpe dicunt, barbare loqui. Greca
80   lingua plus Graecis debet, quam latina Latinis. Non enim illi ita illam
excarnificant, quemadmodum hi hanc. Non facile quis dixerit pre-
ceptores quam graviter peccent, dissimulantes vicia sermonis puerorum, quibus instituendis praefecti sunt et quos mercede docent. Non
85   enim dissimulant vicia nummorum, quos relaturi sunt, si qui adultrini
eis praebeantur.

    12. Queruntur si non referre mercedem sibi debitam, si suis debitis
a pueris fraudentur, si quos adultrinos eis offerant. At nescientes
grammaticam, fraudatores sunt. Fraudant enim discipulos suos num-
90   mis, cum doceant eos mercede loqui barbare. O quam miserabiliter
suis nummis fraudantur, qui mercede discunt barbare loqui.

    13. Tria profecto sunt necessaria orationi latinae : constet, inquam,
ipsa ex vocabulis et latinis et tritis et integris. Non sint in ea viciosae
vocabulorum abusiones.

95   14. Viciosae autem abusiones vocabulorum fiunt cum fraudantur
viciose vocabula suis significationibus : ut cum *dictare litteras* significat
litteras scribere. *Dictare* enim est alicui aliquid scribendum dicere.

    15. Non sint tandem in ea viciosae vel coniunctiones vocabulorum
vel constructiones vel compositiones.

100   16. Orthographiam insuper nescientes fraudatores sunt. Fraudant
enim vocabula aut debitis litteris aut debito sono. Quales sunt, qui
dicunt *perhennis, habundo* ; verum fraudatores vocabulorum !

    17. Quidam fraudant ea significationibus suis ut qui dicunt *dictare*
idem significare quod *scribendo scribere aliquid*, teutonice *dychten*.
105   Unde non sunt eiusdem significationis. Sed *dychten* communius est
quam *dictare*. Unde *dictare* significat *alicui aliquid scribendum* aut
dicendum dicere et significat *toe segghen*.

    18. Grammatica itaque est necessaria omnibus his qui nolunt frau-
dare vocabula. Qui teutonica vocabula fraudat litteris aut sono
110   legitimo, ab omnibus deridetur. Latinorum profecto vocabulorum corr-
uptores nullas culparum suarum penas dant ; usque adeo numerosa mul-
titudine sunt. Licet non minus dignus sit, immo magis, qui ab omnibus
derideatur, qui latia nomina fraudat aut legitimo sono aut litteris
debitis, quam is qui teutonica nomina hisce fraudet. Quomodo rursus

115 is qui teutonica verba corrumpit deridetur ab auditoribus, ita etiam
qui latina vocabula corrumpit ridiculum se facit. Quomodo Teutones
cum gallica verba sermoni suo miscere volunt, ea plerumque corrum-
punt, ita etiam Latini cum greca suo sermoni.

19. Bene loquitur qui neque barbarismo, neque soloecismo, neque
120 viciosa aliqua catachresi sermonem suum viciat.

20. Modi significandi mehercule indigni sunt, qui a pueris discantur.
Credibile est puerorum institutores tam indignos mercede esse, qui
pueros docent modos significandi, quam qui agros filicibus serunt.
Dicant mihi, qui modos significandi laudibus ad sidera tollunt : cui
125 modo significandi debeat infinitivus modus, quod supponat sibi accusativum ? Cui item modo significandi debet *interest*, quod construatur
cum his ablativis *mea, tua, sua,* et cetera.

21. Qui grammatici dicuntur, non ideo grammatici dicuntur quod
sciant modos significandi, sed quia sciunt latine loqui ! Qui negantur
130 esse grammatici, ideo negantur grammatici esse, quia nesciunt latine
loqui, non ideo quia nesciunt modos significandi.

22. Modorum significandi noticia non efficit grammaticum, quia
qui de modis significandi scripserunt ne ipsi quidem grammatici fuere.
Totus enim eorum sermo barbarus est.

135 23. Sola lingua latina est modis significandi fedata. Neque Greca
lingua neque barbara ulla ita fedata est modis significandi, quemadmodum latina. Teutones fatentur hanc orationem teutonicam esse
congruam : *ick byn.* Qui tamen modorum significandi noticia carent !

24. Propterea non negatur quis grammaticus esse eo, quod nesciat
140 amare regere accusativum, quia significat *per modum transeuntis in
alterum,* sed quia nesciat inter grammaticos convenisse ut regeret
accusativum.

25. *Habeo pecuniam* recte dicitur sicut *Careo pecunia. Pecunia
habetur a me* recte dicitur, *Pecunia* autem *caretur a me* non recte
145 dicitur. Non convenit enim inter grammaticos ut diceretur : *Pecunia
caretur a me.*

26. Nonne itaque condolendum est pueris, qui mercede discunt
tam inutilia tamque falsa ? Propterea *Habeo pecuniam, Pecunia* item
habetur a me recte dicitur. Inter grammaticos enim convenit ; ita
150 dicatur. Si convenisset inter grammaticos ut diceretur *Careo pecuniam,*
recte diceretur *Careo pecuniam,* et item recte *Pecunia caretur a me.*
Sed quia convenit inter grammaticos ut non diceretur *Careo pecuniam,*
non recte igitur dicitur.

27. Quare non dicitur *Amo Joannis* sicut *Memini Joannis,* hoc
155 est *Memoriam Joannis habeo.* Nec *Amo Joannis* significat tantum
quantum *Amorem Joannis habeo,* nisi quia non placuit grammaticis
ut *amo* construatur cum genitivo. Placuit autem eis *memini* cum
genitivo construi.

28. Quare Augustinus, Hieronymus, Gregorius, Ambrosius, Barern-
160 dus, Cyprianus et Lactantius et alii ecclesiastici scriptores latine
scripserunt, nisi quia ita scripserunt ut Veteres, hoc est ut Tullius, ut
Salustius, ut Livius, ut Virgilius, ut reliqui Veteres scripserunt ?
qui nec noverunt, nec legerunt Michaelem de Morbosio ! Sed latine
tamen, immo latinissime scripserunt. Ita enim ut Veteres scripserunt.
165   29. Neque eo latine scripserunt, quia sciverunt modos significandi,
sine quorum scientia credunt nonnulli neque latine posse scribi neque
dici. Scripserunt autem latine, quia Veteres imitati et ita ut Veteres
scripserunt.

    30. Ut ille optume pingit, qui ita pingit ut is qui optime pinxit,
170 ille item optime caelat, qui ita caelat ut is caelavit qui optime caelavit,
ita ille optime loquitur, qui ita loquitur ut is loquutus est, qui optime
loquutus. Ita ille optime canit, qui ita canit ut is cecinit, qui optime
cecinit.

    31. Demus itaque operam ut ita loquamur quomodo is loquutus
175 est qui optime loquutus—quem fuisse Tullium inter omnes convenit—
pretermisso itaque barbarissimo illo opere, quod *Scholarium Disciplina*
(Nam satis Latinam inscriptionem non habet !), quod Boetium scrip-
sisse mentiuntur.

    32. Qui libellus tam ineptis tropis refertus est [ut] indignissimus
180 sit quo pueri instituantur. Huic debemus quod dicimus *naturam
naturantem* et *naturatam* ; inde deprompta sunt *magistrari, intitulari,
discolus*. Ibi enim scriptum est : *Non est dignus magistrare qui se non
novit subjici*. Ibi *magistratus* magisterium dicitur. Inde *presbyterari*
formaverunt. *Magistratus,* cum nomen est, Latinum est ; cum parti-
185 cipium, barbarum. Inde depromptum est *dyscholus*, quod significat
malum et perniciosum et toleratu difficilem. Δυσ enim, cum ver[bo]
Greco scriptum, malum significat et *chole* coleram. Inde *discolus*. Inde
depromptum est : *Non enim discentis est probris contumeliosisque affati-
bus regentem incitare.*

190   33. Dicent forte adversarii, qui barbariei partes defendunt : " Fas
quidem est quaedam vocabula secus scribere atque inter Veteres ea
scribi convenit. Fas est vocabula quaedam corrumpere ".

    34. Quibus admissis, fas proinde erit omnia vocabula aliter quam
inter Veteres convenit scribi. Tollatur ergo grammatica, facessant
195 igitur grammaticae professores !

    35. Adherendum vocabulariis et barbaris et corruptis : *Gemmae,*
inquam, (titulo mutato, quo quam multi decepti et decipiantur, non
facile dicetur. Quem unum predicant, quem colunt, qui—ut eis iuveni-
bus fit qui rerum indocti—proprio imponunt ieiunia ventri, aere
200 deficiente !) et ceteris id generis multi : Uguitioni, Catholicon, Britoni ;
relictis et approbatissimis M. Varrone, Festo, Nonio Marcello, tulliano
nestore Tortellio et aliis quam plurimis !

36. Vocabula plane et scribenda et pronuncianda et construenda quomodo inter veteres grammaticos convenit ut vel scriberentur vel
205 pronunciarentur vel construerentur. Qui itaque secus eo vel scribit vel pronunciat vel construit, barbarismum facit.

37. Aeque vocabulis significandum atque inter Veteres convenit eis significari.

38. Quam alienum id a *Gemma* illa, quae circumfertur, videbunt
210 clarissime qui eam approbatis vocabulariis conferant veteribus +consultare+.

[39. Pretereo *Medullam utramque partium, Opus minus* item *utrarumque* et alia opuscula innumera, indignissima qui et emantur et legantur.]

215 40. Frugibus contemptis, glande vesci volunt aliqui non recte persuasi (amore motus haec), in medium nisi maturius studiosa iuventus sibi consulat. Frigido veneno in herbis latente ita cognito, a glandibus itaque fugiant pueri premoniti! *Latet* enim *anguis in herba.* Valete.

NOTES TO PART II, TEXT

l. 2 Non enim propterea . . . ., Fb.
l. 16 Ex quo liquet . . ., Fa, Fb, Fe ; Et quamlibet . . ., Ff, D.
l. 20 tamquam noxia, Fb.
l. 23 determinati, Fb.
l. 29 miseror, Fb ; Ergo misereor, Fa.
l. 33 is aut eis, Fb.
l. 40 perficere, Fa, Fb, Fe ; proficere, Ff, D.
l. 51 Quem coniunctio . . ., Fb.
l. 58 in capitulo . . ., D ; noti recte, Fe.
l. 59 modi, Fe.
l. 60 quod construuntur, Fa (cfr. l. 125 : *quod supponat* ; l. 126 : *quod construatur.* Ergone et heic scribendum : *construantur* ?) ; quod construitur, Fb ; qui construuntur, Fe, Ff, D.
l. 91 frudentur, D.
l. 117 miserere, D ; miscere *scripsimus.*
l. 119 barbarissimo, D ; barbarismo *scripsimus.*
l. 139 negatus, D ; negatur *scripsimus.*
l. 163 Michalem, D ; Michaelem *scripsimus.*
l. 177 Non satis, D ; Nam satis *scripsimus.*
l. 179 Inter *est* et *indignissimus* nos *ut* inseruimus, syntaxeos causa.
l. 186 συσ, D ; ver *compendio scriptum in* D, *inde nos* verbo.
l. 201 Tuliano, D ; tullianus *scripsimus.*
l. 210 conferat, D ; conferant *scripsimus congruitatis causa. Ceterum de latinitate totius propositionis relativae* qui . . . consultare *satis dubitamus. Numquid excidit ? Aut scribendum est :* . . . veteribus. Consultare praetereo . . . ; D *autem sic habet :* . . . conferat. veteribus consultare Pretereo. . . .
ll. 215-216. aliqui non recte persuasii Amore motus. hec in medium . . ., D. *Locus obscurior. Incisum* amore motus haec (scil. : dico) *distinximus non sine dubio. At* motus *neque cum* aliqui *neque cum* iuventus *apte quadrat. De locutione* in medium consulere *videsis Livium* XXIV 22, *15.*

III. Notes

Contra modos significandi :
On the history and linguistic problems of the mediaeval *Modi significandi*
see now :

H. Roos, S.J., *Die Modi significandi des Martinus De Dacia. For-schungen zur Geschichte der Sprachlogik im Mittelalter*, Münster Westf. 1952 ;
J. Pinborg, *Die Entwicklung der Sprachtheorie im Mittelalter*, ib., 1967.
Both works are volumes of the series *Beiträge zur Geschichte der Philosophie und Theologie des Mittelalters*, viz. Band XXXVII, Heft 2 and XLII, Heft 2.

§§ 11-12 : Cf. L. Valla, *Elegantiae*, II, praefatio : . . . *Papias aliique indoctiores, Eberardus, Huguitio, Catholicon, Aymo et ceteri indigni qui nominentur, magna mercede docentes nihil scire aut stultiorem reddentes discipulum quam acceperunt*. . . .

§ 23 : ick byn (in modern Dutch : *ik ben*) = *I am*.

§ 28 : Gregorius certainly is Pope Gregory the Great. The presence of Bernard as the only mediaeval author among the ancient ecclesiastical writers seems a little bit surprising. However, it is not without parallel in praehumanistic works written in the Netherlands : see note 16 of the introduction.

§ 28 : Michael de Morbosio : better is M. de Marbasio. Michael de Marbaix, whose life is almost completely unknown, shortly after 1280 wrote his *Modi significandi singularum partium orationis* or *Summa modorum significandi*, which survives in at least 11 manuscripts of the 13th, 14th and 15th centuries. See J. Pinborg, cit., pp. 90-94 and p. 316 (list of manuscripts) ; Ch. Thurot, *Notices et extraits de divers manuscrits latins pour servir à l'histoire des doctrines grammaticales au Moyen Age*, Paris 1868, quotes several extracts of it ; F. Morand, *Questions d'histoire littéraire au sujet du Doctrinale metricum d'Alexandre de Villedieu, de ses glossateurs et, particulièrement, de Nicolas Francisci*, in : *Revue des Sociétés savantes*, 3e S., II (1863, 2e sem.), pp. 50-57, says that " Mychael de Marbosia, *in suis modis significandi* " was used by the author of a *Doctrinale prosaycum*, viz. Nicolaus Francisci, who seems to work in Brabant about 1430.

§ 31 : *Scholarium Disciplina* : Hegius means the prose treatise *De Scholarium disciplina*, which was generally ascribed to Boethius notwithstanding the fact that its language is clearly late mediaeval Latin. See our introduction and the notes 12-15 for its success in the Low Countries. To these testimonies may be added a letter of Joannes de Veris, written in the *Collegium Lilii* of the University of Louvain, autumn 1466, to a student in Paris, in which a quotation is introduced *Boetio attestante qui ait* : cf. the edition of the text of the letter by G. Meersseman in *Humanistica Lovaniensia*, XIX (1970), pp. 184-185.

The text of the *Disciplina* is edited in Migne, *Patrologia Latina* LXIV (1847), col. 1223-1238. We were not able to ascertain whether the new edition announced by J. Porcher, *Le De disciplina scholarium* : *traité du XIIIe siècle faussement attribué à Boèce*, in : *Positions des thèses de l'École nationale des chartes*, Paris 1921, has been published or not.

naturam naturantem et *naturatam* : cf. cap. III (col. 1229B at the end) : *natura permissione naturantis*.

magistrari : passim, e.g. cap. II (col. 1227B) : *multos vidimus magistrari*.

intitulari : cf. cap. II (col. 1227B) : *paucos inspeximus intitulari* : cap. VI (col. 1236D) : *vidimus strenue intitulari*.

discolus : cf. cap. II (col. 1227A) : *Non sit autem scholaris dyscolus. Dicitur enim dyscolus quasi a schola divisus. Schola enim Graece, dicitur vacatio Latine : inde dyscolus, quasi vacatione divisus. Dyscolus autem dicitur ille qui discurrit per vicos et plateas et tabernas et meretricum cellulas, per publica spectacula, per pompas et choreas et per comessationes et per publicas coenas, et hoc vagis oculis et effrena lingua, petulanti animo, vultu incomposito* ; *omnibus his schola postponitur*.

Non est dignus . . . : cf. cap. II (col. 1226D) : *quoniam qui se non novit subjici, non noscat se magistrari*.

Non enim discentis est . . . : this seems not to be a literal quotation. In chapter II (col. 1227B) one reads : *Ne sit autem discipulus violentus erga magistrum.* . . . *Non est ergo dignus scientia, qui scientiae insurgit praeceptori*.

Magistratus is currently used instead of *magisterium* in the whole work. See e.g. the end of chapter III (col. 1230A) : *Sit ergo discipuli summa magistratui subjectio*.

§ 35 : *vocabulariis* : concerning Latin vocabularies used in the Netherlands during the 15th century, see P. S. Allen, *The Age of Erasmus*, Oxford, 1914 ; H. F. Bouchery, *Latijnsche lexicographie der XVe en XVIe eeuw in de Nederlanden*, in : *De Gulden Passer*, 22 (Antwerp 1944), pp. 69-70 ; K. Grubmueller, *Vocabularius ex quo. Untersuchungen zu lateinisch-deutschen Vokabularen des Spätmittelalters*, München 1967 ; F. Claes, *Latijnse woordenboeken en het onstaan van de lexicografie in de volkstaal*, in : *Hermeneus*, 39 (Zwolle 1967-68), pp. 228-238.

Gemma : a dictionary called *Gemma vocabulorum* was published i.a. at Antwerp in 1494 and at Deventer in 1495, but was already preceded by a *Gemmula vocabulorum*, printed several times between 1484 and 1492, particularly at Antwerp and Deventer. The *Gemmula* contains largely the same words as the *Vocabularius ex quo* of the early 15th century, edited many times from 1467 to 1498 in Germany and the Netherlands. One of these editions was printed at Zwolle in 1479. The *Gemma* was still successful in the first decades of the 16th century. An edition of

Antwerp 1505 calls it *Vocabularius optimus Gemma vocabulorum merito dictus*.

Uguitio : Huguccio of Pisa, grammarian, theologian and canonical writer, became bishop of Ferrara in 1190 and died there on 30th April 1214. One of his works is a systematical and etymological lexicon, called *Magnae Derivationes*, which was largely used during the Middle Ages but never printed. Prof. Marinoni (Milan) is studying it. See A. M. Stickler in : *Lexikon f. Theologie und Kirche*, V (1960²), 521-522 ; B. Bischoff, *Das Griechische Element in der Abendländischen Bildung des Mittelalters*, in : *Festschrift Fr. Dölger = Byzantinische Zeitschrift*, 44 (1951), pp. 27-55, in particular p. 52.

Catholicon or *Summa quae vocatur catholicon* is the name of the most famous mediaeval dictionary by the dominican Joannes Balbi of Genua (+1298), in Latin *De Ianua*. This work, written in 1286, has five parts : orthography ; prosody ; etymology and syntax ; rhetoric and, finally, a vocabulary which is by far the most extensive. The *Catholicon* was largely derived from Huguccio but arranged in an alphabetical order instead of the weary etymological system of its main source. It was printed at Mainz in 1460 and at Lions as late as 1520. See B. Bischoff, l.l., and J. Schmidt in : *Lexikon f. Theologie und Kirche*, V (1960²), 1036.

Brito William (Guillelmus) is the author of a very popular *Summa* or *Expositiones difficiliorum verborum*, written in France about 1250. He is to be distinguished carefully from a younger poet of the same name, who completed an epic *Philippeis* in 1225. The author of the *Summa* wrote also a less well known verse treatise on Greek and Hebrew Words (*Brito metricus*), which has been edited by Lloyd W. Daly, Philadelphia 1968 (*The Haney Foundation Series of the University of Pennsylvania*, No. 2). The same scholar prepares an edition of the *Summa*.

M. Terentius Varro, Roman scholar (116-27 B.C.), who wrote i.a. 25 books *De Lingua Latina* of which 5-10 are partly extant. There are several modern editions : G. Goetz-R. Schoell (Leipzig, Teubner 1910) ; R. G. Kent (London, Loeb Class. Libr., 1938[1] ; revised reprints 1951 and 1958), with English translation, etc.

Festus, Sextus Pompeius, Roman scholar of the late 2nd c. A.D., who epitomized the *De significatu verborum* of Verrius Flaccus (time of Augustus). Only the second half of Festus work survives, but a shortened version made by the Carolingian scholar Paulus Diaconus is completely preserved. Edition by W. M. Lindsay (Leipzig, Teubner 1913, and again in the series *Glossaria Latina*, IV, 1930).

Nonius Marcellus, Roman lexicographer from Northern Africa (East Algeria) in the 4th c. A.D. His work *De Compendiosa doctrina* in 20 chapters or books is still extant but for the 16th. Edition also by W. M. Lindsay (Leipzig, Teubner 1903, 3 vols.).

Tortelli Ioannes, Italian humanist, keeper of the Vatican library and friend of L. Valla, who dedicated to him his *Elegantiae linguae latinae*. He was born, probably at Arezzo, about 1400 and died 26th April 1466. In 1449 he completed his *De Orthographia*, which was printed for the first time at Rome and Venice in 1471. New editions succeeded rapidly at Treviso, Vicenza and Venice during the next three decades. See e.g. Hain, nrs 15563 sqq., and on Tortelli in general : O. Besomi e Mariangela Regoliosi, *Valla e Tortelli*, in : *Italia Medioevale e Umanistica*, IX (1966), pp. 75-189 and XII (1969), pp. 129-196. We wonder if Hegius ever read himself Tortelli's *Orthographia*. Perhaps he knew him only from an addendum to the *Gemma Vocabulorum*. The editions of Antwerp 1494 and Deventer (1495, 1497, 1498) in fact have a section of *Propria nomina clarorum hominum populorum urbium provinciarum montium ac fluviorum magis insignium ex Joanne Tortellio*. If this is true, it would explain why Tortelli is the only Italian humanist cited, although several others were printed or at least known at Deventer in Hegius' life-time : so Valla, Gasparino Barzizza, Sulpicius Verulanus e.a.

Hegius calls Tortelli with some exaggeration a " Tullianus Nestor ", viz. a man speaking as sweet as the Homeric hero Nestor and as elegantly as the Roman orator M. Tullius Cicero.

§ 38 : Perhaps one should put a full stop after *veteribus* and link *consultare* with *Pretereo*, notwithstanding the fact that this last word is printed with a capital in the edition of 1503.

§ 39 : This paragraph is almost certainly interpolated after the death of Hegius, because it mentions books which in all probability appeared only after 1498. Unless we assume that Hegius knew an earlier, now completely lost edition, he cannot have written the text of this paragraph.

The *Medulla* is a commentary on the *Doctrinale* of Alexander de Villa Dei. Its author is Timannus Kemenerus from Werne, near Dortmund, who was appointed rector of the Cathedral school at Münster on Easter-day 1500. See D. Reichling, *Die Reform der Domschule zu Münster im Jahre 1500*, Berlin 1900, p. 22 ; Id., *Zu Timann Kemmener*, in : *Festschrift zur Feier der Einweihung des neuen Gymnasialgebäudes*, Münster in W., Königl. Paulinisches Gymnasium, 1898, pp. 7-9. His commentary was printed at Deventer by Richard Paffraet about 1500 in two parts (hence : *medullam utramque*). The first part bears the following title : *De arte grammatica quattuor partium Alexandri medulla aurea iam emendata et verissimorum vocabulorum interpretatione adaucta precipue eorum in quibus lingua latina apud Germanos longo tempore deficit Que si diligenti revolveris animo quicque hactenus barbarizantium more eructasti iam latina lingua exprimes non minus mature quam lepide*. On p. Aii^r begins a preface which proves that Kemenerus was already rector at the moment he wrote that text : *Timannus Kemenerus Wernensis litterarii ludi Monasteriensium Westvalie magister bonarum litter-*

arum studiosis S.D. The second part is called *Medulla aurea in dia-
sintecticam Alexandri iam emendata et faciliori disposita ordine* : *cum
multis aliis notabilibus in priori medulla omissa.* It begins with the
Epistola in regiminum vires modosque significandi, which we print
hereafter.

On the *Medulla* in general see M. F. A. G. Campbell, *Annales de la
typographie Néerlandaise au XVe s.*, The Hague 1874, nrs 1071-1072,
the date of which is corrected by M. E. Kronenberg, *Contribution to a
New Edition*, ib. 1956, p. 90, on the basis of D. Reichling, *Das Doctrinale
des Alexander de Villa-Dei*, Berlin 1893, pp. LXVII-LXVIII. This
latter reads (p. LXVII, note 2) : *Praetereo medullam* utrarumque *partium*, which is not in the 1503 edition of the invective and cannot be
in keeping with the title of the *Medulla*. In fact, it is *quattuor partium
Alexandri medulla*. Perhaps Reichling was induced here into an error
by the colophons of the two parts (*Finis istius prime partis sive Medulle
Auree* and *Finis secunde partis*) or, more probably, by a false analogy
with the title of the second work in the paragraph, viz. the *Opus minus
utrarumque* (*partium*).

A certain William Zenders of Weert published among other grammatical works a commentary on the same *Doctrinale* in two volumes
called *Opus minus primae partis* and *Opus minus secundae partis* (hence :
utrarumque) *collectum per Wilhelmum Zenders de Werdt.*

According to the *Gesamtkatalog der Wiegendrucke*, Bd I, Leipzig
1925, nrs 1167-1177, the first part was printed two times, the second
nine times. The first edition of the first part, of which only two leaves
survive in the Royal Library at The Hague, seems to be printed at
Gouda about 1490 by Gotfridus de Os. See Wytze and Lotte Hellinga,
The Fifteenth-Century Printing Types of the Low Countries, Amsterdam
1966, vol. I, p. 83 and vol. II, plate 171. The second edition appeared
at Deventer on 26th January 1499 after the death of Hegius. The
second part was printed at Gouda on 16th April 1488, at Cologne about
1490, at Deventer on 9th August 1494 and again two times in 1497.
From all this it is perfectly clear that Hegius probably knew the *Opus
minus* but not the *Medulla aurea.*

§ 40 : Cf. Cicero, *Orator 31* : *Quae est autem in hominibus tanta perversitas
ut, inventis frugibus, glande vescantur ?* These words occur in a context
on style.

Cf. Vergil, *Bucolics III 93* : *Latet anguis in herba.* Notice the striking
coincidence with the last words of Kemenerus' *epistola* !

IV. APPENDIX

TIMANNUS KEMENERUS WERNENSIS

Epistola in regiminum vires modosque significandi

1. Morem legimus professorum fuisse veterem (quem posteri crescentibus
disciplinis imitati) ut veri habendi gratia si quid ab auctoribus perperam

scriptum credidissent, id emendare et corrigere vellent nec vel amicis nec praeceptoribus parcerent, modo veritati subvenirent. Sic Aristoteles Platonem, Varro Lelium, Casellium Sulpitius, Hilarium Hieronymus, rursum Hieronymum Augustinus reprehendit. 2. Alii quoque permulti leguntur, quorum contentione ingenuae artes et illustratae sunt creveruntque maxime. 3. Cum itaque in litterariis gymnasiis pleraque in Alexandrum multiplicataque commentaria et celebrantur et dictantur, non minus eleganter dicta vel parum docte tradita, sed plane falsa et viribus regiminum modisque significandi obstipata, non potui sane pati bona ingenia sic decipi et turpiter errare diutius. Opem tum veritati, tum grammaticis tirunculis ferre volui, in quorum sinu maxima spes et studiorum ratio fovetur. 4. Sic ergo statui diasinteticam restringere Alexandri sicque ordinare ut et excellenti iuvenes ingenio rudesque memoria iusto regiminis ordine, vocum et constructionis dignitatem inveniant quam facillime, omni verborum prolixitate inutilique argumentorum copia in longum solationis annum abiecta. 5. Multae enim res parvi corporis, filioli mei, quae rebus magnis anteferuntur, quaeque multo praeclariores censentur. Res etenim virtute, non magnitudine aestimandae. Quid nam minutius carbuncula ? Quid brevius adamante ? Quid hyacintho magis pusillum ? Nihil tamen his preciosius nobiliusve offenditur. 6. Scribitur in Priapeis (poeta laudans Tideum parvo corpusculo decoratum, +nam+ tamen maximum viribusque ingentissimum) :

Utilior Tideus, qui, siquid credis Homero,
Ingenio pugnax, corpore parvus erat. (*Priapea*, LXXX 5-6).

Et a Papinio non minus vere quam diserte dictum :

Maior in exiguo regnabat corpore virtus. (Statius, *Thebais*, I 417).

7. Quis umquam librum extulit eo quod magnus foret ac copiosus ? Quis orationem existimavit verbosam enormemve lepidam et venustam ? Quis poma ob magnitudinem ubertatemque legit unquam ? Nemo, per Herculem vel modice eruditus id accesserit ! 8. Laudamus quippe codices disertos, eruditos, doctissimos, concinnatos. Hi magnis anteponuntur voluminibus, quibus nulla inest eruditio nullave facundia. 9. Caveant igitur bonarum artium studiosi a commentariis sane magis prolixis, argumentosis suasionibus exhaustis, modis significandi diffusis. Efficaciam nempe loquendi et lepide, vehementiamque scribendi et sincere haud docent. 10. Vidimus enim quamplurimos verborum prolixitati adherentes longius quam latinae linguae iuvenes fere om / Aii^v / ni bonarum litterarum studio qui nondum eloqui (taceo dicere) ceperunt. 11. Proh pudet haec scribere magisque pudet bonas mentes sic decipi. Quid enim, per Deum immortalem, reprimeret adolescentem maturum et etate et ingenio non ea brevi sapere et memoria revolvere quae debite limateque iam tradita de grammatices preceptis. 12. O quantulocumque spacio nectariam illam dulcedinem verborumque elegantiam, orationis structuram, dicendi generum varietatem, sententiarum tandem dignitatem invenirent longissimo tempore perditam, si huius artis rudimenta, accidentium distinctionem, partium ordinationem, vero ac

Library • St. Joseph's College
222 Clinton Avenue
Brooklyn, N. Y. 11205

perfecto accentuum pondere singula quanto clarius quantove absolutius investigarent ! 13. Quid plura ? Noticiam vires regiminum minus efficiunt grammaticam. Prestantissimos cernimus viros, qui vires regiminis non gustarunt. Finis grammatices recte loqui recteque scribere auctor est Quintilianus (*Instit. Orat.*, I 4), quem vis regiminis minime docet. 14. Regimen orationis unum aut multiplicatum viribus rerum non causatur. Varias enim haec exempla *dux aulae, tunica Conradi, vas vini* evomunt vires vel modos significandi, unum tamen regimen relinquunt. Quid itaque nos cruciamus ut virium diversarum apicem consequamur, quae nihil facundiae, nihil eloquentiae nobis conferunt nec denique quemque litterario provocant sermone. 15. Si etenim vis dicendi in his alienis a vera grammatices traditione facultatibus lateret, Donatus, Servius, Diomedes, Priscianus, Vectoinus (*sic* !) ceterique huius traditionis viri et eruditi et eloquentes modorum significandi debilitatem haud tacuissent, qui nihil huius artis dignum pretermiserunt.

16. Fugite igitur, o preclara ingenia, fugite ! *Frigidus latet anguis in herba* (Vergilius, *Bucol.*, III 93) !

NOTE TO PART IV, APPENDIX

We copied this text from the first edition of the second volume of the *Medulla Aurea*, f. Aii^r-^{v}, at the Royal Library of The Hague. Punctuation marks and references to the authors quoted are ours. To make understanding of the text easier, we always put *ae* instead of *e* in flexional endings. The original printing has *e*. We corrected the following misprints : (1) Arestoteles ; (6) deserte ; (7) copiosius ; perhercule (or is this a false word-formation after the type Mehercule ?) ; (8) nulla*n*e ; (12) quantilocumque.

We left untouched the *crux* in § 6, although it is fairly sure that one should read *animo* instead of *nam*. In § 9 we wonder if one should read *magnis, prolixis* (which makes a good sense) instead of the quite irregular comparative *magis prolixis*. Finally, the name Vectoinus in § 15 no doubt hides the Roman grammarian Victorinus.

P.S.—When this article was in the press, Prof. Ch. Béné (Grenoble) drew our attention to some attacks on the " modistæ " by the Alsatian humanist J. Wimpfeling, viz.
(1) *Isidoneus Germanicus* (Strassburg 1497), ch. XXI, *De lectione poetarum et oratorum*, ff. xlv^r-xv^v : seducti enim a suis praeceptoribus, qui Alexandrum, Floristam, Cornutum, Catholicon, Petrum Heliae *significandi*-que *modos* cum argumentis dubiis et quaestionibus eis perplexe inculcarunt . . . ; f. xvl^r : Proh dedecus ! O temeritatem ! Mavis apud Alexandrum, Floristam, Cornutum, Joannem de Carlandria (*sic* !) *modosque significandi* in veteri nos barbarie . . . sordescere quam ex poetis et oratoribus Romanam linguam . . . inter nostrates disseminari.
(2) *Pro concordia dialecticorum et oratorum* . . . *oratio* (1499 ; copy at Zürich, Stadtbibl.), p. Aiv^r : . . . sciat quispiam omnem Alexandrinam grammaticam, sciat omnes regulas, sciat omnes *significandi modos* : nisi habeat electa vocabula, nisi clausulas habeat latinas, numquam copiosus erit in dicendo. . . .

J. IJSEWIJN

Louvain

II

NOTES ON THE COMPOSITION AND RECEPTION OF GEORGE BUCHANAN'S PSALM PARAPHRASES

Buchanan's metrical paraphrase of the Psalms was quite extraordinarily successful. Before his death in 1582, sixteen editions had appeared, not counting selections ; by 1600 another twenty had been brought out, and since that date some sixty editions have been printed. This is only an approximate figure : there may still be some editions to add to the list, while others, whose existence is vouched for by respectable sources, are still to be accounted for. There are also over twelve editions of the *Poemata* that include the paraphrases ; various selections have appeared as well as a number of translations into various languages, though chiefly into English. The history of these editions poses many problems : the early printings vary considerably in their text, as Buchanan changed his mind on many readings up to the time of his death ; and there is also the question of the relationship between these editions. Much remains to be ascertained about the motives that prompted Buchanan to undertake his paraphrase, and also about the sources, classical and contemporary, on which he drew. In this essay, I shall devote more space to the early period ; my description of later editions will be intentionally succinct. My concern is to present the material in more orderly fashion than has hitherto been the case and to suggest lines which might be explored in more detail.[1]

[1] The first attempt to establish a bibliography will be found in the Ruddiman edition ; I use the 1725 Leyden edition of the *Opera omnia*, in two volumes, henceforth described as *OO*. P. A. Budik, *Leben und Wirken der vorzüglichsten lateinischen Dichter des XV-XVIII. Jahrhunderts*, 3 vols., Vienna, 1828, gives a bibliography in II, pp. 248-52. The two modern bibliographies are : J. Maitland Anderson, " The Writings and Portraits of George Buchanan, *George Buchanan 1506-1906 : A Memorial*, St Andrews, 1907, available in off-print, 22 pp. ; and, more thorough, often with location of volumes, that prepared by David Murray in *George Buchanan : Glasgow Quatercentenary Studies*, Glasgow, 1907. The section on the paraphrases covers pp. 407-29.

The following abbreviations have been used to designate libraries where copies of the Paraphrases are to be found ; my list of locations is not complete, nor is it meant to be so, but some further information will be found in Pollard & Redgrave, *STC* 1475-1640 and Wing, *STC*, 1641-1700 ; also in J. R. Naiden, *The Sphera of George Buchanan* (1506-1582), Philadelphia, 1952, pp. 157-65.

A = Aberdeen University ; Amst = University of Amsterdam ; Ant = Plantin-Moretus Museum, Antwerp ; B = The Queen's University, Belfast ; Br = Brechin Cathedral Library (at present housed at the University of Dundee) ; BM = British Museum ; BN = Bibliothèque Nationale, Paris ; C = Cambridge University, with additions in brackets, where necessary, to indicate College libraries : Cai = Gonville and Caius, Chr(ist's), Corp(us), Emm(anuel), K(ing's), Tr(inity) ; D = Trinity College, Dublin ; E = Edinburgh University ; E(NC) = New College, Edinburgh ; F = Freiburg ; G = Geneva, Bibliothèque Publique et Universitaire ; GM = Mitchell Library, Glasgow ; GU = Glasgow University, with (m) to denote the Murray Collection ; L = London Library ; M = Rylands Library, Manchester ; NLS = National Library, Scotland ; O = Oxford, Bodleian, with additions in brackets, where necessary, to indicate College Libraries, A(ll Souls), C(hrist)C(hurch), C(orpus Christi), M(agdalen), N(ew College), Q(ueen's), S(t John), W(adham), Worc(ester) ; StA = University of St Andrews ; StA(hf) = Hay Fleming Library, St Andrews ; V = Versailles.

Our knowledge of the way in which the paraphrases reached their definitive form will probably remain fragmentary. As we have very little manuscript evidence, we must rely chiefly on remarks scattered in the Correspondence, occasional contemporary references and the variants introduced gradually into the early editions. In his *Vita*, the humanist makes only brief allusion to the composition of the Psalms, undertaken during his confinement in a Portuguese monastery :

> Hoc maximo tempore Psalmorum Davidicorum complures vario carminum genere in numeros redegit.[2]

and they are presumably included in the statement he made on the publication of some poems undertaken after the return to Scotland :

> Eo reuersus nomen Ecclesiæ Scotorum dedit. E superiorum autem temporum scriptis quædam velut e naufragio recollecta edidit.[3]

Nor did Buchanan provide a prefatory letter to the first edition ; we must therefore look elsewhere for clues.

Though Buchanan's confinement in Portugal may have offered the main stimulus to composition, he had had ample opportunity to acquaint himself with the genre in his earlier years of residence in France. The first complete Latin verse paraphrase of the Psalms appeared in 1531 from the pen of François Bonade, a prolific writer of orthodox poetry ;[4] more important, in all probability, was the taste for psalm paraphrase among Neo-latin poets whom Buchanan must have known, if not personally, at least through their writings : Salmon Macrin and Nicolas Bourbon, poets who knew Greek, were in the vanguard of pedagogic reform and had evangelical leanings.[5] During the 1540s, the work of two foreign humanists enjoys much success in France : on the one hand, the paraphrases of Eobanus Hessus, which

I should like to express my gratitude to colleagues who have kindly given me information and advice : Mr D. MacArthur, University Librarian, St Andrews ; Dr R. Donaldson, National Library, Edinburgh ; Miss Hester Black, Glasgow University Library ; Mr B. J. Roberts, British Museum ; Mademoiselle Agnès Joly, Bibliothèque Municipale, Versailles ; Dr S. S. B. Taylor, University of St Andrews ; Mr C. Morgan, Bodleian.

[2] The most easily available edition is James M. Aitken, *The Trial of George Buchanan before the Lisbon Inquisition*, Edinburgh and London, 1939, p. xxv. The *Vita* is also printed in *OO*, I, fol. g^v-i 4^v.

[3] Aitken, op. cit., p. xxvii.

[4] *Eximii prophetarum antistitis regia Dauidis oracula*, Paris, Wechel, 1531 (Copies : BM, BN). On this author see R. Lebègue, *La Tragédie religieuse en France. Les Débuts 1514-1573*, Paris, 1929, pp. 123-8. On the Psalm paraphrases as a genre, see H. Vaganay, *Les Traductions du psautier en vers latins au XVIe siècle*, Freiburg, 1898 ; J. A. Gaertner, " Latin verse Translations of the Psalms 1500-1620 ", *Harvard Theological Review* XLIX (1956), pp. 271-305, and the complement-article in the same review, " Neo-latin verse translations of the Bible ", LII (1959), pp. 205-11. On the genre in the vernacular see Michel Jeanneret, *Poésie et tradition biblique au XVIe siècle*, Paris, 1969 ; and Clément Marot, *Pseaumes*, ed. S. Lenselinck, 1969.

[5] Macrin published his *Septem Psalmi in lyricos numeros* . . . in Poitiers in 1538, not very long after his Low Country friend Cornelius Musius had printed some paraphrases in the same town. Macrin also wrote other paraphrases scattered in more miscellaneous volumes, such as the *Hymorum libri sex* and the *Odarum libri sex* that both appeared in 1537. Nicolas Bourbon's *Nugarum libri VIII*, Lyons, 1538, also contains some paraphrases.

went through a number of editions,[6] and on the other, the *Explanatio* and thirty paraphrases of Marcantonio Flaminio ;[7] his writings were admired by Marguerite de France, who afforded Buchanan some protection after his return from Portugal.[8] More significant from our point of view are the 75 paraphrases published by Jean de Gagnay in 1547,[9] not only because this author provides us with the theory of the genre, but because Buchanan had some connection with him at this very time :

> Offerebant mihi in Gallia amplas condiciones Abbas Iveriaci homo nobilissimus qui me etiam in morbo pecunia benigne iuuerat, in Vasconibus item Episcopi Tarbellensis et Condomensis, in aula regia Card. Lotharing. et Card. Guiniacensis (sc. Guise) et Franciæ Cancellarius suasu Jo. Gagnei theologi et Lazari Bayfii quorum domestica consuetudine usus sum aliquot menses in aula.[10]

These various paraphrases must of course be seen against the background of scholarly interest taken in the elucidation of the Psalms in a period of religious ferment. In addition to the works I shall mention below,[11] there were the prose translations and paraphrases of which Campensis' (1533) was perhaps the most popular in France ; the paraphrases of Raynerius Snoygoudanus (1536, Cologne ; 1538 Lyons ; 1542 Antwerp ; 1545 Paris ; 1559 Lyons, and later printings) ; Franciscus Titelmann's *Elucidatio in omnes Psalmos* (Paris, 1545) and Bucer's translation and explanation of the Psalms, published originally in 1529 and reprinted at Basel in 1547. Marot's Psalms had appeared before Buchanan left for Portugal, and, if, as is possible, the Scotsman was connected with the court of Marguerite de Navarre,[12] here would be another source of stimulus. Finally, the study of Hebrew had been singularly developed by François Vatable, whom it is extremely likely that Buchanan knew ; as we shall see later, there is circumstantial evidence to suggest that he drew on Vatable's scholarship.[13]

In our present state of knowledge, we have early manuscript versions of only five Psalm paraphrases and of the *Hymnus matutinus*, usually added to the full set of psalms. Moreover, these manuscript sources, which probably belong to the 1550s, do not differ substantially from the first selection printed in 1556, though fortunately two of the psalms in manuscript state were first published later. Our first source is a Vatican manuscript which

---

[6] Already very popular in Germany (1538 Marburg ; 1539, 1542, 1544 Strasbourg), Eobanus' paraphrases were also published in France : 1547 and 1549, Paris ; 1557 Lyons ; 1565 Paris, etc.

[7] The *Breuis explanatio* appeared in 1546, the paraphrases in 1546 in Venice. There are French editions from 1546 onwards.

[8] See Buchanan's preface to his 1556 edition of the *Alcestis*.

[9] *Psalmi Davidici Septuaginta quinque in lyricos uersus redacti*, Paris, 1547 (Copies : BN, C, O). On Gagnay's conception of the paraphrase, see below pp. 56-7).

[10] J. M. Aitken, op. cit., pp. 28-9.

[11] See below, pp. 58 ff.

[12] See I. D. McFarlane, " George Buchanan and French Humanism ", *Humanism in France at the end of the Middle Ages and in the early Renaissance*, ed. A. H. T. Levi, Manchester U.P., 1970, p. 307.

[13] See below, pp. 58 ff.

contains the text of Ps. I, XV and CXXVII (= CXXVIII).[14] I shows two variants :

> v. 2 ... sed magni decreta patris rimatur et alta
> (becomes 1565 ?, first edition, referred to subsequently as A,
> ... sed vitae rimatur iter melioris)

and in v. 5 a line on which Buchanan continued to hesitate :

> Aura leuis torquet rapidis ludibria ventis.

This reading, maintained in 1556, will have the ending changed to *celeri ludibria vento* in A and early editions, but later to *vacuo ludibria coelo*. XV, which is very short, has more variants proportionately :

> v. 1 Augusta coeli templa quis incolet
> Tecum sancte parens ? ...
> becomes in A
> Stellata coeli templa quis incolet (later Sanctae Sionis ...)
> Rex magne tecum ? ...
> v. 2 excors (A expers) ; granda (A grata)
> v. 4 decipit (A despicit) ; suspexit (A suspicit) ; promissi est (A omits est).

CXXVIII has two minor variants in v. 3 : grauido (A grauidi) and domo (A domum), but in v. 4 a more important one :

> Sic tempora transiget   (A Quem timor Domini tenet)
> Inter talia commoda
> Quem timor Domini tenet   (A Vitæ tempora transiget).

The variants introduced into A were subsequently maintained in all other editions. These variants, though not of great moment, show Buchanan's concern with the choice of epithet and of case (determined by the context of agreement).

The other manuscript versions occur in a BN volume which contains many different *états* of profane poems :[15] the two psalms in question are XLIX and LXV, and unfortunately present only minor differences (XLIX, v. 4, *sinu* for A *penu*, v. 6, *trudat* for A *ducat*, v. 7, *inspice* for A *adspice* ; LXV, v. 9 *Turbidum* for A *Turgidum*, v. 14 *opaca* for A *amica*), but the text of the *Hymnus matutinus* is markedly different. In the first place, the second stanza is missing, as is also the case in the early editions, and second, there are several lines that will undergo considerable change :

> l. 9 Offuscat (A Iam fuscat, later Sed offuscat)
> l. 10 crassa (also A ; later nostra)
> l. 12 Mentes tenebrae contegunt ... (also A ; later Mens pene cedit obruta)
> l. 14 Mundoque da diem suum (also A ; later Diemque da mundo suum)
> l. 21 irrigatus (also A ; later irrigetur).

---

[14] Vatican, lat. 6246, fol. 116r-117v. I refer to *OO*, II, for the " standard " version of the paraphrases ; but it is difficult to speak of a " definitive " text.

[15] BN, fonds lat. 8140 (*G. Buchanani Varia Poemata*), fol. 59v-62.v On this and other manuscripts see I. D. McFarlane, " George Buchanan's Latin poems from Script to Print—A preliminary Survey ", *The Library*, Fifth series, XXIV (1969), pp. 277-332.

In l. 9 Buchanan probably wanted to avoid alliteration ; in ll. 12-13 the antithesis between *tenebris* and *sol* seemed no doubt effective, but the insertion of the second stanza, with *tenebris* in the final line, compelled the omission of the same noun in l. 12. Line 14, with its altered order, reflects Buchanan's liking elsewhere for separating two words that agree with each other.

Not so very long after the Scotsman had returned to Paris from his stay in Coimbra, Henri Estienne persuaded him to offer some paraphrases for a volume he was then editing.[16] In order to represent the various countries, he chose two authors from Italy, Flaminio and Ravizza (Rapicius), and one from the other countries, Eobanus Hessus whose success we have mentioned, Salmon Macrin whom Estienne included out of patriotic necessity rather than by literary criteria, and George Buchanan to whom the liminary letter is addressed. Estienne also inserted some Greek paraphrases by Paul Dolskius and himself. The letter reveals his great admiration for a scholar on whose services he was to draw again ;[17] and he published nineteen of Buchanan's versions, I-XV, CXIV, CXXVII (= CXXVIII), CXXXVII, and, after the *errata*, in a note to the reader, CIV :

> . . . Caeterum quum psalmum CIIII Buchanani summi (nec tamen pro merito) laudassem, eo placuit libellum hunc claudere.[18]

When Estienne approached him, there would presumably be little difficulty in extracting the early paraphrases of the series, though it is not certain Buchanan worked that way ; what about CIV and the later ones ? Had he completed the set, or nearly so, in some preliminary state, and if so, why were these particular ones selected ? Was it that Estienne liked them especially, or did it suit his book to match them with those of Macrin who of course had not published a complete set ? If Macrin was to be allowed a fair place—only II of his appears among the first fifteen—, selection of the later psalms might be determined in part by two criteria : choice of psalm which had been attempted by Macrin as well as by the others, and an adequate literary standard. But nothing is certain here.

The Buchanan paraphrases that belong to the main text are laid out, with the exception of the latter part of IX, on the left-hand page, and may be followed by versions from other hands. On the right-hand page Estienne has printed paraphrases of the same psalms by other writers : thus, VI begins on pp. 26 and 27 ; Buchanan's version is set out on p. 26 and on p. 27 stands Flaminio's ; to follow, p. 28 provides Rapicius' and p. 29 that by Eobanus Hessus.

---

[16] *Davidis Psalmi aliquot Latino carmine expressi.* A quatuor (sic) illustribus poetis : quos quatuor regiones, Gallia, Italia, Germania, Scotia, genuerunt. . . Ex officina Henrici Stephani. An. M.D. LVI. (Copies : BN, E, O).

[17] See my article, above-mentioned, in *The Library*, pp. 287 and 313-4.

[18] *Davidis Psalmi* . . . p. 94. D. Irving, *Memoirs of the Life and Writings of George Buchanan*, Edinburgh, 1807, p. 124, says that the version of Psalm CIV " might alone have conferred upon him the character of a poet ".

26

Buchanan's versions were obviously well thought of by other umanists, because they were reprinted in Léger Duchesne's *Flores* four years later, with the exception however of CIV, which had evidently escaped the anthologist's notice. The 1556 version of CIV contains a few variants worth mentioning :

v. 1   The opening line shows, once again, Buchanan's preoccupation with word order :
> Te Deus alme canam rerum . . . (also A; later Te rerum Deus . . .)

v. 11 Pascua (also A ; later Pabula)

v. 14 erumpat (A onwards assurgat)

v. 25-26 . . . per stagna liquentia cauda
> Veliferas circumnant puppes. . .
> (The intermediate line : Exsultant : tot monstra ingentia & horrida visu is missing, but is supplied from A onwards)

v. 32 Aspiciente (A onwards Concutiente)

v. 35 Rex (A onwards Deus).

Duchesne's anthology has a *privilège* of 16 February 1554 ; the first volume is dated 1555, but the second volume, entitled *Farrago*, did not appear until 1560.[19] The anthologist, a royal reader and a near-contemporary of Jean Dorat, had published his first volume, the *Flores epigrammatum* in 1536, and the 1555 edition reproduces most of the poets originally represented. In the second volume, apart from some Italian poets, the authors are for the most part humanists well-known to Duchesne himself, Adrien Turnèbe, Elie André, Claude d'Espence, Germain de Brie (who, though he died in 1537, is probably retained because he had been one of Duchesne's teachers), Michel de l'Hôpital, Joachim du Bellay, Jean Girard, Nicolas Chesneau (Querculus), Jean Dorat and Duchesne himself, whose *Prælectiones* had appeared in 1549. A great number of the poems selected are of an encomiastic or ceremonial nature, which no doubt explains the presence also of Buchanan's *De Caleto recepta*, very welcome at a time when so much Latin verse is connected with the Guise entourage. Buchanan's paraphrases are retained in their numerical order, with the exception of II and III, which, omitted " nescio quo casu ", had to be added at the end of the section.[20]

Several of these psalms, whose text naturally does not vary from that given by Henri Estienne in 1556, show no great divergence from the definitive versions ; we have already looked at I, XV and CXXVIII ; XI remains unaltered and in XII the variant *aurae* for *aure* is probably a misprint. Very often—I am not giving a full list of alterations—Buchanan changes one word : III, v. 6, *voce* (A onwards *nocte*) ; v. 7, *cuncta* (A onwards *sæua*) ; V, v. 5, *pura* (A onwards *vera*), v. 12 *At* (A onwards *Sed*). Sometimes, the order is altered : VI, v. 11 *Tristi ut repente* (A onwards *Tristi, repente ut*) ;

[19] The second volume carries the title : *Farrago poematum ex optimis quibusque et antiquioribus et ætatis nostræ poëtis selecta* per Leodegarium a Quercu . . . Parisiis, apud Aegidium Gorbinum, 1560. (Copies : BM, BN.)

[20] The main series of paraphrases will be found fol. 158r-169v, Psalms II and III on fol. 170r-v ; and the *De Caleto recepta* on fol. 171r-172v.

or there will be a modification of the parts of speech : VI, v. 4, *Grauisque mentem mœror* (A onwards *Mentemque grauiter*) ; Buchanan's known hesitation on moods is shown in II, v. 12, in the change from *sint* to *sunt* (A onwards). There may be more substantial modifications :

II, v. 5   Et vi furoris cæca consilia sui
            (A onwards Et per furorem cæca consilia suum)

VI, v. 8   Obtusa longis, & hostium (A onwards Hebetata longus : hostium)

XIV, v. 2   Nec cuiquam studium est recta capessere (A onwards Nec quisquam ex animo recta sequi student)

CXIV, v. 4   Lætaque frondosi mouere cacumina colles
            (In the early editions, Lætaque remained, but frondosi was changed to frondentes ; from 1580 we have Celsaque instead of Lætaque.)

In all this, one can see certain principles at work, and I have mentioned one or two, to which one should add the preference for a word of less pagan resonance, the search for a more satisfactory epithet, or indecision in the use of particles and conjunctions.

It may also happen that the paraphrase appears satisfactory to Buchanan until after the early editions, when he decides to modify the text to suit his developing taste. Thus he introduced only minor alterations into the text of VII in A (v. 2 *sœua* for *lœua* ; v. 15 ; *ærumnam* for *ærumnas* ; v. 16 *ruit* for *ruet*), but from 1580 onwards, the whole of v. 5 and part of v. 15 are replaced. This is also true of VIII, v. 8 and IX, vv. 7-9 which are greatly modified in 1580 ; and in X, vv. 4 and 5 are not merely altered, but reduced from twelve lines to six. Such major alterations appear to occur precisely in the psalms which first appeared *hors série* ; it seems that Buchanan was not prepared to revise, except in details, psalms published before A, but that he later became more critical of his first fruits. One other question arises about the Duchesne set of paraphrases : why in fact did the humanist include Buchanan in his anthology ? No doubt, literary distinction was one of the factors in the reckoning ; he was also one of Duchesne's colleagues, in that he held posts in various Paris colleges both before and after his journey to Portugal. Furthermore, if one looks at the list of collaborators, one will notice that they nearly all belong to those humanist poets who were closely linked with Michel de l'Hôpital and the Cardinal de Lorraine, at a time when ceremonial Latin poetry becomes a marked feature of the literary landscape.[21] There may be one other factor, since Duchesne was an ardent Catholic, to the point of fanaticism : he might be very glad to include among his chosen authors a humanist who had certainly brushed with ecclesiastical authority, but who in recent years seemed to have come to terms with the religious establishment and whose presence on that account would be welcome.[22]

[21] After a series of meagre years, 1558-60 see the appearance of an impressive number of Neo-latin *plaquettes*.

[22] On Buchanan's religious attitudes, see my article in *Humanism in France* (mentioned in note 12), pp. 306-11.

In 1560 or thereabouts George Buchanan returned to Scotland in circumstances which still remain to be clarified ; and though he soon declared his sympathy for the Calvinist Church, he did not in any way break yet with Mary Queen of Scots, whose court poet he was to remain for some time. We are very badly informed about these years, so far as the Psalms—and indeed many other circumstances—are concerned. The one clue is to be found in a letter from David Rizzio to Jean de Morel, dated 31 May 1564 :

> Je n'ay failly de faire voz recommendations à Monsieur Buccanan qui vous en rend ung million, et s'il eust parachevé le livre de psaulmes en vers latins come il a comencé il m'en eust faict part pour les vous envoyer. Mais il m'a promis que vous serez le premier prefferé aprez qu'ils seront parfaictz.[23]

This quotation shows that Buchanan did not finish his paraphrases until quite soon before they were published by Henri Estienne ; it also suggests that Paris friends were still eagerly awaiting the appearance of the whole series ; and it finally dispels the view advanced by earlier writers that the manuscript of the Psalm paraphrases was in Estienne's hands as early as 1562 :

> That famous printer is represented as having long deferred the impression ; and it is at least certain that the manuscript was in his custody so early as the year 1562. Its suppression might be imputed to various causes : but according to the very learned Hadrianus Junius, he had protracted the edition with the secret view of claiming this version as his own, in the event of Buchanan's decease. Many circumstances render this supposition highly improbable.[24]

Henri Estienne certainly had access to various manuscript sources of Buchanan's poems, since he uses some unpublished texts of the " profane " poems in his *Apologie pour Hérodote* ;[25] but Buchanan was, by then, needing continual prodding to get his verse into print—and one may wonder whether Charles Utenhove, whom he described as " censor meorum carminum " in 1564,[26] did not have a hand in putting the finishing touches to the psalms as well as to the profane poetry.

The first edition of the Psalms appeared from the printing house of Henri and Robert Estienne without place or date of publication :

> PSALMORVM / Dauidis paraphrasis poetica, / nunc primùm edita, / Authore Georgio Buchanano, Scoto, poe- / tarum nostri sæculi facilè principe. / Eiusdem Dauidis Psalmi aliquot / à Th.B. versi (sc. Theodoro Beza Vezeliense). / *PSALMI ALI-/quot in versus itē Græcos nu- / per à diuersis translati.* / Printer's device / Apud Henricum Stephanum, & eius fratrem Robertū Stephanum, ty- / pographum Regium. / EX PRIVILEGIO REGIS.

---

[23] BN, ms. lat. 8589, fol. 39-40.

[24] D. Irving, op. cit., p. 119.

[25] See references in note 17.

[26] The phrase occurs in a poem addressed by Buchanan to Utenhove ; it is reprinted in *OO*, II, pp. 281-2, and is dated " nonis Juniis 1564 " in a manuscript of the Camerarius collection, Staatsbibliothek, Munich, vol. 33, fol. 310ʳ·ᵛ.

8°. 18,5 × 10,8 cm. * iiii, a-r⁸, s⁴, a-c⁸. In two parts separately paginated : (viii) + 277 pp. + 3 blank pp. ; 46 pp. + 2 blank pp. Main text roman. Gardy 228.[27] Copies : BM, C, C(K and Tr), G, GU(m), M, NLS, O, O(E and P), StA, V.

The volume is variously given in library catalogues as printed in Geneva or Paris ; Buchanan, of course, had a number of his early publications printed in Paris ; many of his friends anxious to see him in print had been active in the French capital, and the statement " Ex privilegio Regis " seems destined for a French audience, but the evidence is perhaps not conclusive. The problem of the date is also tiresome. That this edition is the first, seems incontrovertible : the *errata*, listed on p. 277, have all been incorporated in the text of the 1566 edition. We have a *terminus a quo* in the letter of David Rizzio from which I have just quoted ; and a *terminus ad quem* can be established by the date of the six-year *privilège* granted by Philip of Brabant to Christophe Plantin and printed at the beginning of his 1566 edition :

> . . . datum in Privato Consilio viii. Martij. Anno. M.D.LXV stylo Brab.

This suggests that the first Estienne edition must have come out sometime in 1565, or at the latest, in the spring of 1566.

One or two features of this edition should be mentioned. Though Buchanan had pride of place, his was by no means the only contribution : Bèza's paraphrases ran to some ten pages only, but the Greek versions take up nearly forty pages : they include renderings by Henri Estienne himself, Florent Chrestien,[28] Frédéric Jamot[29] and an anonymous contributor. The section of liminary verse, in both Latin and Greek, was substantial : it contained a Pindaric ode by Jamot, other poems by François Laporte and Estienne, and the Latin poems, with the exception of an epigram by Lodoico Castelvetro[30] and a distich " incerti authoris ", were from Estienne's pen. The tributes to Buchanan were handsome, but in the volume Estienne was also very concerned with the promotion of things Greek. The Psalms were presented quite simply with the *incipits* of the Vulgate, and three other poems accompanied them : the liminary lines dedicated to Mary Queen of Scots, written therefore before their break, the *Hymnus in Christum*, which

---

[27] F. Gardy, *Bibliographie des Œuvres . . . de Théodore de Bèze*, publ. avec la collaboration d'Alain Dufour, Geneva, 1960 (*THR* XLI). Some of Buchanan's profane poetry also appeared with works by Bèze. So far as the psalms are concerned, Gardy gives Geneva as the probable place of printing.

[28] A monograph on this French humanist who wrote in French Latin and Greek, is badly needed. Much of his work remains manuscript (e.g. Rasse des Nœux and Dupuy Collections, BN). According to a note by Daniel Rogers (fonds Dupuy, vol. 951, fol. 52ʳ), Buchanan wrote a liminary poem for Chrétien's edition of the Pseudo-Denys, of which no copy is at present known.

[29] Jamot studied in Paris ; later he published some Neo-latin verse that shows the influence of Jean Dorat.

[30] Whether Buchanan met Castelvetro in Italy is not known ; on the other hand, the Italian spent the years 1564-6 in Geneva, and Estienne may have persuaded him to contribute to the edition.

usually is printed with the paraphrases but had not reached its definitive form,[31] and the epigram against pilgrimages (*Epigramma in quo imago introducitur alloquens peregrè aduenientes*).[32]

Before we look at the second Estienne edition, we might settle the matter of the Strasbourg editions printed by Rihel and based on the edition just described. The first of the Rihel series appeared in 1566 :

PSALMORVM DA- / VIDIS PARAPHRASIS POETICA, / nunc primùm edita, / AVTHORE GEORGIO BVCHANANO / Scoto, poetarum nostri sæculi facilè / principe. PSALMI ALIQVOT IN VER- / *sus item Græcos nuper à diuersis* / *translati.* / Printer's device / *Anno* M.D.LXVI.
12°. 11.5 × 7 cm. BB-CC⁴, A-C⁸, D⁴-E⁸ . . . . Y⁴-Z⁸, a⁴-b⁸ . . . e⁴-f⁸. xvi + 352 pp. Title page in red and black type. On p. 352 Colophon : ARGENTORATI / Excudebat Iosias Rihelius. / M.D.LXVI. Copies : BM, BN, F, StA.

As a derivative edition, it merits only brief comment. Though reference to them was excluded from the title-page, the Bèze paraphrases were incorporated,[33] and indeed the whole Estienne text stands, but the corrections noted at the end of the edition have been introduced into the text here. That this edition was a success is shown by the number of printings that followed from the house of Rihel.[34] The next appeared in 1568 : the title was the same, except that one sentence was added : *Annotata ubique diligenter carminum genera*, which means that Rihel had simply borrowed a feature from the Plantin edition recently issued.[35] This section follows the paraphrases on pp. 281-7 and at the same time takes the place of the epigram

---

[31] The St Andrews copy of this edition has, added in hand, the later variants of this hymn.

[32] This epigram was suppressed in Catholic editions, but its original place was probably in the *Fratres fraterrimi*, where Ruddiman includes it, *OO*, II, pp. 284-5 ; the Baluze ms 280 (BN) includes this poem ; but though that ms was the one almost certainly used for the first edition of the *Franciscanus* and accompanying poems, the epigram was in fact omitted before or at the printing stage. C. Utenhove inserted it in his edition (Guarinus, Basel, 1568), but it is only from 1584 onwards that it is normally included with the *Fratres*. The date of the first Estienne edition may be fixed within a narrower margin by the following quotation from Claude d'Espence whose allusion is dated *Lutetiæ ex ædibus Rhemœis, ineunte Anno* 1566 :
    Sed & omni versuum genere Psalmos & sacra Cantica plures incluserunt, in tanto nimirum hodiernorum ingeniosorum prouentu : idem Bonadus, Flaminius, Spinula, Hessus, Rapicius, Salmonius, Ganeius Theologus, & cuius nobis hæc lucubrantibus in lucem exiit, poëtica paraphrasis, Buchananus, dicas lyræ aureæ plectrum eburneum, modulis adeo scitis, & omnium hactenus dulcissimis pulsat & personat.
(from *De Diuina sacrorum Bibliorum & patrum poesi*, in *De Collectarum in Ecclesia Latina origine, antiquitate* . . ., *Opera omnia quæ superstes adhuc edidit.* . . . Paris, C. Morel, 1619, p. 1032. This work was first published, according to Cioranescu, in 1566).

[33] Hence, no doubt, why Gardy does not mention this edition.

[34] Rihel, it appears, had already published in 1567 Buchanan's versions of the *Alcestis* and the *Medea* in *Tragœdiæ selectæ Aeschyli, Sophoclis Euripidis*. I have not seen a copy, but it is presumably a reprint of Estienne's volume published in the same year at Geneva.

[35] 8°. 13,5 × 8,5 cm. * ii, A-X⁸. iv + 336 pp. (Copies : BN, O, St A). The size given in cm is approximate, as measurements are affected by binding requirements, etc.

on pilgrimages. As in the Plantin edition, the *carminum genus* is also indicated below the *incipit* of each psalm. The format is different and the text has been reset with a consequent change in pagination. One final point : though the Greek paraphrases are maintained (pp. 289-336), the Bèze paraphrases have quietly vanished.

In 1572, yet another edition came out, with the title suitably enlarged to take account of a new feature :

PARAPHRASIS | PSALMO= | RVM DAVIDIS POETICA. | NVNC PRIMVM EDITA, | Authore Georgio Buchanano Scoto, poëtarum | nostri sæculi facilè principe. | *HIS ADIECIMVS M. ANTO- | nij Flaminij argumenta, in singulos | Psalmos* : *ITEM,* | PSALMOS ALIQVOT IN VERSVS | Græcos nuper à diuersis translatos. | Annotata ubiq3 diligenter carminum genera. | Printer's device | CVM GRATIA ET PRIVILEGIO. | M.D.LXXII.
8°. 11,75 × 7,25 cm. A-Y⁸. 348 + 4 blank pp. Colophon : ARGEN-TORATI | Excudebat Iosias Rihelius, | M.D.LXXII.
Copies : A, C, C(K), NLS, O.

Flaminio's *argumenta*, already successful enough in other countries, became sufficiently popular for Rihel to maintain them in his later editions. In 1575, he brought out another printing, which apart from the date, appears identical with the 1572 one (Copies : M, NLS, StA). The final edition of this series was published in 1578, and though Rihel adds nothing of great interest to the textual tradition, this issue does differ in various respects from his previous pattern : this edition appears to be very rare, and the only copy I know is in the Murray collection, Glasgow University ; it belonged formerly to Tobias Reichenbach and then to Ioannes Mihályhájs. Its title-page, whose wording is the same as the 1575 issue, down to " in singulos Psalmos ", it is in 12° ( ) : (⁸, A-X⁸; xvi + 336 pp.). All the Greek elements have vanished, including such liminary verse as was couched in Greek ; in its place some additional liminary material has been introduced, from scholars of Silesian origin :

) : (iiiij v GEORGII FABRI= | *CII CHEMNICENSIS* | IVDICIVM DE VERSIONE | Buchanani.
CITHARAE DAVIDI= | *CAE ENCOMIVM, M. GE=* | ORGII CALAMINI SILESII. (94 ll. in elegiac couplets)

Calaminus (Roehrich) was a professor at Linz and translated Euripides but he is less well-known than Fabricius who had made a name for himself as a scholar and poet with strong Calvinist convictions. His *Ars poetica* was widely read ; some of his early works were published in Paris and he was certainly influenced by J.-C. Scaliger. Whether Buchanan ever corresponded with him is not known, but it is interesting to find this eminent humanist lending his authority to the psalm paraphrases ; and the Silesian features in this edition suggest a further spread in the popularity of Buchanan's work. Though this edition, as we have seen, is not a simple copy of the 1575, it appears too early for certain latterday variants to be included.

32

We can now return to the mainstream and look at the second Estienne edition, which this time carried the date of printing :
PSALMORVM / Dauidis paraphrasis poetica. nunc / primùm edita, / Authore Georgio Buchanano, Scoto, poë- / tarum nostri sæculi facilè principe. / EIVSDEM BVCHANANI TRA- / *gœdia quæ inscribitur Iephthes*. / Cætera eius opera seorsum edita sunt. / Printer's device / ANNO M.D.LXVI, / Apud Henricum Stephanum, & eius fra- / trem Robertum Stephanum, ty- / pographum Regium. / EX PRIVILEGIO REGIS.
16°. 12, 75 × 5, 75 cm. i-ii + A-S⁸. iv + 284 + 4 blank pp.
Copies : Ant, BM, BN, C, C(Chr. and Tr.), GU(m), L, NLS, O(two copies, one lacking the *Jephthes*), O(C, CC, Q, Worc.), StA.

The liminary verse of the first edition is dropped, and so are the Bèze paraphrases ; and though the corrections listed in the first edition are introduced into the text, there are no other textual modifications. One may wonder why the Estiennes were prompted to publish the paraphrases in a different format and presentation so soon after the first edition ; perhaps the fact that Rihel was doing all that was necessary is sufficient explanation, but the Estiennes may have felt that the addition of the *Jephthes* would increase the market attraction of the volume, especially for those who were interested in Buchanan's paraphrases, but less so in the Greek renderings. The *Jephthes* had already gone through two Paris editions (1554, 1557) before the outbreak of the wars of religion ; but, though Buchanan's attitude to the problem of vows appears to have been orthodox—and Plantin will have no difficulty in including the play in his early editions—, there is no doubt that the *Jephthes* becomes extremely successful in Reformation countries and is seen by some as an attack on a Catholic principle on which Calvin had had a good deal to say in his *Institution*. Admiration for the play did, however, transcend sectarian boundaries;[36] and the Estiennes set a pattern for many later editions, by adding the play to the paraphrases. After Buchanan's death, editions will often carry both the *Jephthes* and the *Baptistes* which, though written at about the same time at Bordeaux, was not published until 1577.

Buchanan himself was not entirely satisfied with the Estiennes' presentation of the paraphrases, as is evident from a letter to Pierre Daniel dated 24 July 1566 :

In Psalmos multo typographorum errata correxi, quædam etiam mea non pauca mutaui : quamobrem velim cum *Stephano* agas, ne me inconsulto id operis iterum emittat.[37]

[36] Florent Chrétien's translation into French of the play was extremely successful : 1567 Orléans, 1573 Paris, 1581 (Geneva), 1587 Paris (with works by Des Masures) with reprint in 1597. Another translation had appeared by Claude de Vesel in 1566—the author marked the choruses as being sung to Psalm tunes ; at the beginning of the XVIIth century there are two other French renderings : André Mage de Fiefmelin (Poitiers 1601) and Brinon (Rouen, 1614). Translations were also published in other countries : Strasbourg 1569, Nürnberg 1571, Cracow 1587, Lucca 1587 (repr. 1600), Budapest 1590, Rostock 1595, Brunscwick 1604. There have been several English versions since the XVIIIth century.
[37] *OO*, II, p. 724.

Buchanan may have been thinking more particularly of the first edition, but the second was not impeccable, and the Estiennes will not publish another edition for nearly ten years. On the other hand, the early Estienne editions become the source for the first ones to come from the press of Christophe Plantin, who had acted very speedily to obtain his *Imprimatur* after the paraphrases had appeared from Estienne. There is no evidence that Plantin, keen though he was to print anything Buchanan had to offer of a suitable nature, was in direct communication with him at this time ; in our present state of knowledge everything points to Plantin's having worked on the Estienne editions. This is clear, not only from a comparison of the actual editions, but also from the existence of a copy of the 1566 Estienne volume which is now preserved in the Plantin-Moretus Museum, Antwerp, and which was used by the printer to set up his own edition. On p. 50, a marginal correction supplies *opis* which had been inadvertently omitted by the Estiennes. On pp. 234-5, the offending epigram on pilgrimages has been deleted, and the text of the *Jephthes* refoliated by hand for the printer's benefit, so as to take into account the space left by the epigram. On p. 255, there is a mark against the line *Tuius tremendus & seuerus hostibus*, and on p. 284 the *Imprimatur* by Schellinc is reproduced in manuscript.

Within a very short time, Plantin succeeded in publishing two editions of the Paraphrases. The first one came out in 1566 :

PARAPHRASIS / PSALMORVM / DAVIDIS POETI- / CA, NVNC PRIMVM / EDITA, / Auctore Georgio Buchanano, Scoto, / poëtarum nostri sæculi facilè principe. / *Adnotata ubique diligenter carminum genera.* / EIVSDEM Buchanani tragœdia / quæe inscribitur Iephtes (*sic*). / Printer's device / ANTVERPIAE. / Ex officina Christophori Plantini. / rule / CIꝐ. IꝐ. LXVI. / CVM PRIVILEGIO.
16°. 11,5 × 7,5 cm. a-v⁸ + α-γ⁸. 318 + 1 unnumb. + 3 blank pp. + separately paginated second section (containing the Greek texts), 46 pp. *Approbatio* on p. (319).
Copies : Ant, C, C(Cai. and Emm.), The Caius copy does not have the separately paginated Greek section.

This edition was destined for a Catholic audience, hence the removal of the epigram on pilgrimages. What was new in this issue was the addition of a section on the *Carminum genera* (pp. 261-5) which shows that Plantin had immediately recognised the pedagogic potential of the paraphrases. In this, he sets an example which will be extensively copied ; he also indicated the *genus* in the heading to each psalm. The Greek section, though it contains the same number of pages as the Estienne edition, is freshly printed (and the gatherings carry Greek characters for their signatures) ; so that Plantin has in fact conflated the first two Estienne editions, since the *Jephthes* is also included.

Though Plantin does not seem to have been in direct touch with Buchanan at this time, a common friend Van Giffen (Gifanius) acts as some sort of intermediary, and on 17 Cal. Feb. 1567 writes to the Scotsman about the Antwerp printer :

Est vir ille dignus, quem & tuis versibus adjutes & studio : ille jam
Psalmos tuos elegantissime, formis suis descripsit, & nihil aliud fere,
quam tua ardet suis typis expolire.[38]

In Plantin's Correspondence there is a reference to the printer's sending a
copy of the Psalms to a friend, together with an Epistle of Clénard and the
Adagia of Erasmus, on 8 August 1566.[39] In the following year, van Giffen
again keeps Buchanan in touch with developments in Antwerp ; as is made
clear in his letter to Plantin (25 June 1567) :

> Accepi hodie duas litteras a Dn. Buchanano et Raverdo duobus
> praestantissimis Scottiæ viris. Miserunt una qæe petieram epi-
> grammata. Ea omnia una cum epistola nunc ad te mitto, videbis
> ipse quod scribunt. Rescripsi illis nudius tertius, petiique ut psalmos
> suos mittat, te paratum esse illos jam statim excudere. Misi quoque
> ad eum psalmorum eius tuam editionem secundam, ut laudent tuam
> diligentiam. . . Oraui quoque summopere Buchananum ut opus de
> Sphæra tibi quoque tradat.[40]

Van Giffen is referring of course to the Plantin edition that came out in
March 1567 :

> PARAPHRASIS / PSALMORVM / DAVIDIS POETICA, / MVLTO
> QVAM ANTEHAC / CASTIGATIOR, / Auctore Georgio Buchanano,
> Scoto, poë- / tarum nostri seculi facilè principe. / *Adnotata ubique
> diligenter carminum genera.* / EIVSDEM Buchanani tragœdia quæ /
> inscribitur Iephthes. / Printer's device / ANTVERPIÆ, / Ex officina
> Christophori Plantini. / rule / M.D.LXVII. / CVM PRIVILEGIO.
> Colophon : ANTVERPIÆ EXCVDEBAT / CHRISTOPHORVS
> PLAN- / TINVS, ANNO M.D.LXVII. / MENSE MARTIO.
> 16°. 12 × 8 cm. A-Z[8], a[8]. 379 + 5 unnumb. pp. Main text italic.
> The psalms are numbered every five lines, and not by versicles, as
> will so often be the practice.
> Copies : BM, BN, NLS, O. There is a slightly different issue of this
> edition, BM.

This edition adds nothing to the corpus, except in so far as an attempt is
made to correct errors, of whose presence Buchanan had complained in the
Estienne editions. In the Plantin correspondence, there is a letter from
Gaspar de Portnarios (of Salamanca) asking Plantin to let his agent Snr
Diego de la Pena have fifty copies of the paraphrases ; and as this letter is
dated 17 July 1569, the reference is presumably to this edition.[41] Plantin
brought out another printing in August 1571, but though the type has been
reset, there are no textual differences from the 1567 issue (Copies : BN,
Freiburg, C(Tr.), StA).

We have evidence that Buchanan and Plantin were in correspondence
at the beginning of the 1570s and that the Antwerp printer would be glad
to print more of the Scotsman's works[42] ; payments appear also to have been

---

[38] *OO*, II, pp. 725-6 (written from Orléans).

[39] *Correspondance de Christophe Plantin* publiée par Max Rooses, Antwerp-Ghent,
III, 1883, p. 9. This date gives a *terminus ad quem* for the first Plantin edition.

[40] Ibid., I, p. 112.

[41] Ibid., II, p. 61.

[42] Ibid., II, p. 141.

made to Buchanan, but in no clearly specified context; and Plantin will not publish another edition of the Paraphrases for over ten years. This does not of course mean that the Paraphrases were unsuccessful, far from it, for by 1572 the Estiennes, Rihel and Plantin had between them produced eight editions, that is an average of more than one a year. Bèza wrote to express his warm admiration :

> Ego Psalmorum tuorum lectione incredibiliter delector : qui etsi tales sunt, quales a te uno proficisci potuerunt. Opto tamen ut eos, quod tibi minime difficile fuerit, ex bonis etiam optimos reddas, vel, si mauis, optimis, quales iam sunt, meliores.[43]

Admiration tinged with a desire for improvement; in this Bèze was unwittingly echoing Buchanan's own thoughts, and it is indeed during this decade that the Scotsman shows dissatisfaction with some of his renderings. Some of his friends must have become aware of his views, for Pierre Daniel, writing towards the middle of the decade, concludes his letter thus :

> In Psalterio si qua mutaueris, quaeso mitte.[44]

The letter is undated, but one wonders whether it is not connected with the edition that Robert Estienne brought out in 1575 :

> PSALMORVM / DAVIDIS PARA- / PHRASIS POETICA. / Authore Georgio Buchanano, Sco- / to, poetarum nostri sæculi facilè principe. / *Eiusdem Buchanani tragœdia quæ / inscribitur* Iephtes. / Printer's device. / LVTETIÆ, / Ex officina Roberti Stephani. / M.D.LXXV.

16°. 11,75 × 7,25 cm. A-Y[8]. 348 + 2 blank pp. (numbering of pages affected by the repetition of 159, 160). Main text italic.
Copies : A, C,[45] NLS, StA, V.

This is not a simple reissue of an earlier edition ; the type has been reset and the pilgrimage epigram omitted. However, the text is otherwise unchanged : the metrical layout of CV and CXXIX, to be modified in subsequent editions, is as before, and the printer had obviously not yet received any textual changes from Buchanan, who had, we have seen, asked Estienne not to republish the paraphrases without his blessing. On the other hand, Pierre Daniel had acted earlier as Buchanan's intermediary in dealings with French printers, and the quotation from his undated letter might have been prompted by Estienne wanting to find out whether any changes ought to be made ; and if Buchanan had not answered promptly, Estienne may simply have gone ahead. But the position is far from clear.

In the same year, Estienne brought out another volume involving the Paraphrases : Jean de Serres published a series of Greek renderings of the Psalms, inspired by Buchanan's Latin example, and printed twenty-four of his paraphrases in parallel with his own.[46] The author, a staunch Calvinist,

---

[43] *OO*, II, p. 733 (letter dated Geneva, 12 April, 1572).

[44] *OO*, II, p. 734.

[45] In the catalogue, this volume is dated cca. 1566, as the title-page is missing and also lacks the *Jephthes* ; but it seems to be a copy of the 1575 edition.

[46] *Psalmorum Dauidis aliquot metaphrasis Grœca*, I. Serrani. Adiuncta e regione paraphrasi Latina G. Buchanani . . . 1575. (Copies : BM, BN which lists two separate issues, C, GU (m), NLS, StA).

had written to Buchanan some time back, but had received no reply ; but he wrote again, some years after the book had come out :

Monsieur, Il y a long temps que je vous honnore, comme font tous ceux, qui aiment les lettres, & si n'ay encore eu ce bien de vous cognoistre, que par vos doctes escrits. Cette année pour addoucir la douleur de nos miseres, & mesmes après ceste remarquable calamité de la S. *Barthelemy* je me mis, en suyvant vos traces, a faire parler grec *David* : combien que je recognoisse que le premier coup d'essay ne me donne ouverture pour passer plus outre, comme de faict je n'en ay poinct affecté de louange, me contenant du bien que j'avois senty de ce remede parmy mes ennuis.[47]

The success of the Paraphrases is not proved only by the number of editions or literary exercises inspired by them as was Jean de Serres' ; evidence is also afforded by the reactions in the Catholic camp. Génébrard's work on the Psalms had been prompted in part by Bèze's efforts in that field, but another author wished to provide verse Paraphrases that combined poetic ability, Hebrew scholarship and the right religious " observatio ". In 1575, an Italian, who had lived for some time in France, published his own paraphrases ;[48] and they were successful enough to go into another edition in the following year. What is interesting here is the prefatory letter written by the printer Fédéric Morel to justify the enterprise, and it is clear that Buchanan's reputation in this field was one of the factors taken into account when Morel published Toscano's version :

Multi antea insigni doctrina viri Psalmorum libros Latinis versibus expresserunt : ex horum numero sunt Eobanus Hessus, Adamus Siberus, Georgius Buchananus, & is qui omnium nouissimus huic operi manum admouit, Benedictus Aria (sc. Arias Montano's version printed by Plantin in 1574). Sed quamuis & hi & alij præterea nonnulli non ultimi nominis Poetæ, piam, Christianoque homini dignam operam nauarint, adeo ut ex iis aliqui summis in cœlum tollantur laudibus : nihilo tamen minus licere arbitror, adhuc eandem materiam versibus complecti : cum id a veteribus tum Græcis cum Latinis factitatum esse nemo sit qui ignoret. . . Piget enim eorum qui nimium poeticis pigmentis addicti adeo subinde longo ab Hebraica sententia interuallo feruntur, ut non modo versus integros, verumetiam integras quandoque periodos de sua addant. sibique placeant, si quid ab ipsius autoris menta alienissimum valeant comminisci, hi sunt qui Cererem, & Bacchum, & Fortunam, & Sortem & Fatum, aliaque impiis tantum gentibus nota nomina sacris poematis impudentissimè inserunt.

The problem of harmonising a pagan idiom with Christian sentiment is one that comes to exercise both Catholic and Calvinist consciences ; nevertheless, behind Morel's prose there lies a desire to produce something that can hold a candle to the paraphrases (nearly all of Reformed inspiration) that have so far appeared.

---

[47] *OO*, II, p. 742.

[48] Giovanni Matthaeo Toscano, *Psalmi Davidis ex hebraica veritate latinis versibus expressi*. Paris, F. Morel, 1575. Second edition 1576, from which I quote, fol. a vii ʳ·ᵛ.

Another indication of Buchanan's popularity is the appearance in 1579 of the first attempt to set his paraphrases to music ; only the first forty-one psalms are involved, but the volume is a very interesting one :

> PSALMI DAVIDIS / A G. BVCHANANO VERSIBVS / EXPRESSI : NVNC PRMVM / MODVLIS IIII. V. ET VIII. VOCVM, A. I. SER-VINO / DECANTATI . . . LVGDVNI / Apud Carolum Pesnot. / M.D.LXXIX.

The musical character of the Psalms had been long recognised, and Bucer had had something to say on the matter some fifty years earlier :

> Odam ego reddidi (i.e. the Hebrew term), alij Psalmum ; sed eruditis significat Psalmus sonam citharae. Ad instrumenta certa decantatos Psalmos, nemo est qui nesciat, sed sic, ut modulatio organorum animum pararit ad percipienda plenius verba sacri carminis.[49]

Servin's work was published in five parts in oblong quarto, but it is now extremely difficult to come by. The only complete copy of which I have knowledge in a public library is to be found in Trinity College, Dublin, but Seymour de Ricci mentions another in Lord Amherst's Library, bound with the arms of James VI of Scotland to whom the author addresses his prefatory letter.[50] I have seen some partial copies elsewhere : the *bassus* is preserved in BM, C and NLS, while St Andrews possesses a portion of the tenor (fol. B-Z⁴, Aa-Cc⁴, Dd-Ee²). Liminary verse was provided by Corneille Bertram, who in the following year was to publish his *De politica Iudaica* at Geneva. I leave it to competent musicians to assess the musical value of these settings.[51]

With the 1580s we enter a new phase in the history of the Psalm paraphrases. We have noted Buchanan's uneasiness developing during the previous decade over the text of some of his renderings. In an important letter sent to Daniel Rogers towards the end of 1579, he wrote :

> In Psalterio quædam correxi, plura atque etiam integros Psalmos mutaturus, nisi ætas ingravescens iamdudum mihi extorsisset Poëmata.[52]

The results of his change of mind are reflected in the next three editions of the psalms to appear, two in 1580 and one in 1582.

We have seen that Estienne's 1575 edition showed no real progress on the previous issues ; his 1580 volume is a very different matter :

> PSALMORVM / DAVIDIS PARA- / PHRASIS POETICA. / Auctore Georgio Buchanano, Sco- / to, poetarum nostri sæculi facilè principe. / *Eiusdem Buchanani tragœdia quæ inscribitur Iephthes.* / Omnia multò quàm antehac emendatiora. / Printer's device / LVTETIAE,

---

[49] In his elucidation of the *Sacrorum Psalmorum Libri quinque*, published in 1529, reprinted in Basel, 1547 (under pseudonym Aretius Felinus), *Præfatio*, fol. α 6 ᵛ.

[50] S. de Ricci, *A Handlist of a Collection of Books and Manuscripts belonging to the Right Hon. Lord Amherst of Hackney at Didlington Hall, Norfolk*, Cambridge U.P., 1906, Nᵒ 302. Other editions of Paraphrases in this library are the first Estienne edition, Plantin 1566, Vautrollier 1580.

[51] G. Bell, " Notes on some music set to Buchanan's paraphrases of the Psalms ", *George Buchanan, Glasgow Quatercentenary Studies*, op. cit., pp. 333-45.

[52] *OO*, II, p. 755.

/ Ex officina Roberti Stephani, / Typographi Regij. / MD.LXXX. 16°. 12,25 × 7,25 cm. A-X⁸, Y⁴. 2 unnumb. pp. + pp. 3-334. Main text italic.

Copies : BN, C, NLS, StA.

Estienne has clearly taken note of Buchanan's injunction not to print the paraphrases again in their original text, but I have not discovered how he got hold of the revised text : the names of Pierre Daniel and Daniel Rogers, as possible intermediaries, spring to mind, but there is no firm evidence to confirm this possibility. Major alterations have been introduced in VII, v. 5, LXXVIII, vv. 21, 22, 24, CX, v. 3, CXXIX, v. 6, CXXXII, v. 6, to mention only a few ; CV and CXXIX are presented in their definitive metrical layout ; LIX, v. 10, omitted in earlier editions, has now been added ; and there are many minor alterations (e.g. L, v. 12, *gremio triformi* becomes *gremio capaci*). Curiously enough, the substantial change of text IX, vv. 7-9, which appears in the other editions of the early 1580s, has not been introduced ; nevertheless, this is a very marked advance on Estienne's 1575 edition and shows his clear wish to bring his text up to date. The printer has not followed Plantin's example of adding the *carminum genera*.

The other edition to come out in 1580 is also extremely interesting : on the one hand, it is the first edition to appear in England, and indeed in Great Britain, and on the other, it contains certain readings which are not found elsewhere. The publisher, Thomas Vautrollier, was a French Huguenot who had moved to England during the 1560s, but his career this side of the Channel was not without incident. It is he who publishes the first edition of the *Baptistes* in 1577, and during the years 1580-6 he is based in Edinburgh, though his wife runs the London press in his absence. He was in touch with Daniel Rogers, who gave him a letter to hand to Buchanan :

> Dedi autem in mandatis integerrimo viro *Vautrollerio* harum litterarum latori, ut exemplaria quædam mihi isthic comparet, ut cum amicis communicarem. . . Quod si respondisses, quid de nostra in Poëmatum tuorum editione sententia (de qua superioribus meis literis tecum egi) judicares, *Vautrollerius* quædam ex ipsis, si non omnia, typis mandasset : nunc intacta iacent, donec quid de ordine in iis imprimendis observando statueris, perspectum habeat : qua de re rectissime cum eo ipso coram nunc egeris.[53]

Vautrollier, therefore, had the opportunity of meeting Buchanan, and it is very likely that his edition of the paraphrases was based on material supplied by the author himself : this would certainly explain the variants which are not to be found in other editions :

> PARAPHRASIS / PSALMORVM / DAVIDIS POETICA, / MVLTO QVAM ANTE- / HAC CASTIGATIOR ; / Auctore Georgio Buchanano, Scoto, poë- / tarum nostri sęculi facilè principe. / *Adnotata vbique carminum genera.* / EIVSDEM Buchanani tragœdia quæ inscribitur Iephthes. / Printer's device / LONDINI, / Excudebat Thomas Vautrollerius, / Typographus. / 1580.

[53] *OO*, II, pp. 751-2.

16°. 11,5 × 7 cm. A-Z⁸. 3 unnumb. pp. + pp. 4-374. Main text italic.
Copies : BM, BN, C, StA. The StA copy is imperfect, as it lacks gatherings F and L (pp. 97-112 and 161-76), as well as the last 110 lines of the *Jephthes* (p. 368 onwards).[54]

Vautrollier had taken some features from the Plantin editions ; the *carminum genera* and the numbering of the text every five lines ; but his text was more recent. He incorporated the variants mentioned in the 1580 edition of Robert Estienne, but also introduced the new version of IX, vv. 7-9 ; on the other hand, there are several readings which appear to be unique to his edition. For instance, XLVIII, v. 8 ran in earlier editions :

> . . . ut æquora
> Verrens, ab imis penitus exitum vadis,
> Trepidas carinas dissipat . . .

Estienne 1580 changes the middle line to

> Excita ab imis penitus everrens vadis

which is the standard version in later editions, except for *everrens* (for *evertens*) ; but Vautrollier has

> Undas ab imis penitus attollens vadis.

It is a line rich in Vergilian echoes and Buchanan may have hesitated on the amount of classical echo he wished to allow. In CXXXII, v. 18, Vautrollier has a separate reading for the penultimate line :

> Florebit cingantque sacrum diademata crinem

which in other editions runs :

> Florebit, cingetque sacrum diademate crinem

There are other variants of a minor character, such *Luctus per* & *suspiria* (for usual *Per luctus* . . .) in XXX, v. 11, and *Rex magne* for *Regina* in XLV, v. 18, a reading that recurs in Julius' edition, London, 1620.

One might have thought that Plantin's edition of 1582 would do little else than reproduce the 1580 editions, but there is some evidence to suggest that he too relied on manuscript sources for at least a few readings :

PARAPHRASIS / PSALMORVM / DAVIDIS POETICA / MVLTO QVAM ANTE-HAC / CASTIGATIOR ; / Auctore Georgio Buchanano, Scoto, poëtarum nostri sæculi facilè principe. / Adnotata vbique diligenter carmi- / num genera. / Printer's device / ANTVERPLÆ, / Ex officina Christophori Plantini. / M.D.LXXXII.
Colophon : ANTVERPLÆ EXCVDEBAT / CHRISTOPHORVS PLAN- / TINVS, ANNO CIƆ, IƆ. LXXXII. XIX. KAL. MART.
16°. 10,5 × 7,75 cm. A-S⁸. 285 + 1 unnumb. pp. Main text italic.
Copies : BM, NLS, O, StA.

Grosso modo, Plantin's text was very similar to Estienne 1580 ; it is more in details that he differs from other editions of the time :

> XXXI, v. 11, for which we saw Vautrollier had a separate reading :
> Plantin has *Mœrore fracta* & *luctibus*, a reading which Ruddiman will later accept as standard.

---

[54] The BM has a second copy with a slightly different title-page, *Typis Thomœ Vautrollerij & impensis Herculis Francisci.*

40

LIX, v. 18 Plantin has *arx ut œnea*, whereas the others have *ut arx œnea*. The Plantin reading is accepted by Ruddiman, on the grounds that the other is metrically unsatisfactory.

CLIX (Heth) Whereas the other editions until then had *me comparo*, Plantin has *me confero*. This reading tends to become ' standard ', but A. Julius, 1620, will still maintain the older reading.

These three editions constitute a milestone in the textual tradition of the paraphrases; they have slightly different elements, though we have no means of knowing how these differences were transmitted to them. If they all came more or less directly from Buchanan, they would suggest that the Scotsman was hesitating almost until his death on the most suitable reading for certain lines. And this hesitation would certainly explain why later editions continue to vary on such points as I have mentioned. These three editions appear to be the last ones which were probably authorised in some degree by Buchanan himself. Robert Estienne did not in fact reprint his edition, but the other two did. Vautrollier brought out another issue in 1583 ; it appears to be extremely rare—the only copy I have seen is in O— and is a straight reprint of the 1580 edition. Plantin published an edition in 1588, which also seems fairly rare : there is a copy in the BN and two more may be found in GU(m). It appears that the Syston Park Library held a beautifully bound copy from the library of Marguerite de Valois ; but it does not add anything of textual value to our knowledge ; Plantin has by now adopted the standard practice of numbering by versicles. David Murray refers to a Plantin edition of 1591,[55] published at Leyden, but I have yet to see a copy. Raphaelengien, Plantin's son-in-law, brought out another edition in 1595, which included the *Jephthes* and, as one would expect, the section on the *carminum genera* (Copies : NLS, StA). The 1603 edition appears to be a simple reissue (Copy : C, erroneously listed as printed in Geneva). In 1609, Raphaelengien brought out two editions, both with the *Baptistes* added : the first has the same pagination as the 1603 and 1609 issues until the *Baptistes* is reached, and there is also added a Hymn by Prudentius (Copy : BN) ; the second is in much smaller format and has 285 pp. compared with the 445 pp. of the first, but it does not include the Prudentius hymn (Copy : BM).

It would be suitable to mention here an edition which never saw the light of day, which has not, so far as I am aware, been preserved in manuscript, but which would have been of considerable value, since the editor-to-be was Alexander Morison, a kinsman of Buchanan. J. J. Scaliger, whose father had known Buchanan in his Bordeaux days, refers in his *Opuscula*, published posthumously in 1610, to this edition. Ruddiman was unable to find any trace of it ; in the B. N. ms. lat. 10327, fol. 156ʳ, is Scaliger's epigram which forms part of a collection of material associated particularly with

[55] D. Murray, op. cit., p. 413.

the circle of Henri de Mesmes, who himself had been instrumental in collecting some of Buchanan's poetry for publication :

> In nouam editionem paraphrasis Buchanani in psalmos, quam Alex.
> Morison. sororis eius filius procurauit.
> Ista Caledonij vertit quę musa poetæ,
>   Iam prius Hebręa carmina culta lyra,
> Typographi primum fœdis damnata lituris
>   Vati nuper erant inficienda suo.
> Excoluit Morison, et doctus auunculis illis
>   Quod dederat, non est passus abesse decus.
> Gaudete, ô summi Vatis, pia numina, Manes,
>   Si noua cognati : vos benefacta iuuant.
> Nunc opus hoc, Morison, quod luminis edit in nouas
>   Vestrum est ; Typographus fecerat ante suum.[56]

In the margin there is a later note : " On ne l'a pas encore imprimée " and on fol. 155 v, that is, just before the poem above, is to be found an unsigned 14-line *Epitaphium G. Buchanani Scoti*. It would seem that Morison's edition had reached a fairly advanced stage, if what looks very much like liminary verse had been composed for it.

There is no doubt that the Paraphrases were well established before Buchanan died ; there is proof enough in the editions I have already mentioned, and to that evidence one may add the testimony of two admirers. Elie Vinet, a very old friend of his, wrote to him not so long before his death and informed him of the success his poetry and plays were enjoying in France :

> Quos vero libri tui fratres dicis, nescio, quorum desiderio teneri possim : sed Tragœdiæ, Psalmi, Elegiæ, Epigrammata Georgii Buchanani, hic prostant.[57]

In the countries of the Reformation, of course, the paraphrases were beginning to attract a large audience, but they did not pass unnoticed in Italy either. Nancel, the biographer of Pierre de la Ramée, who had known Buchanan at an earlier stage in Paris, sent a letter which the Scotsman never received, for he died before it arrived :

> Tantum enim fama tui nominis apud me valet, nulli ut maiorum Poëtarum eximiorum conferre non audeam ; si scribendi stylo quibusdam summis ac primariis priscis illis (licet admodum paucis) supparem, at ipso argumento, & materiæ dignitate (de Psalmis Davidicis intelligo, paraphrasi Poëtica abs te decantatis) longe omnibus illis superiorem ac præstantiorem : ut mihi quidem Spiritus Sanctus (absit dicto invidia) dum Davidis Psalmos vario metro, eoque elegantissimo, & concinnitudine aptissimo, Latine exprimis & effers, tuum genium animare, tuum pollicem impellere, tuam argutam chelyn pulsare videatur.[58]

---

[56] *Opuscula varia antehac non edita*, Paris, Adrien Beys, 1610, p. 287. The epitaph in the B. N. ms. is also by Scaliger, op. cit., p. 286.

[57] *OO*, II, p. 767.

[58] *OO*, II, p. 769. The letter is dated " Turone, Idibus Martiis, 1583 ".

One would expect that Switzerland would wish to follow other countries in printing editions of the paraphrases, and this begins to happen from 1581 onwards, though it is by no means certain that Buchanan's authority was sought beforehand. The first edition is in fact a parallel presentation of the paraphrases by Buchanan and Théodore de Bèze, some of whose paraphrases had accompanied the first Estienne edition of Buchanan's versions. The complete set of Bèze's paraphrases was first published in 1579 (Gardy, No. 229) ; so successful were they that four other editions came out in the same year, two at Geneva, one in Antwerp and one in London, from the press of Vautrollier. Bèze sent a copy of his paraphrases to Buchanan with a letter, dated 10 March 1580 : it is unsigned, but its attribution cannot be in doubt :

> Mitto autem ad te quoque istius libelli exemplar, id est, noctuas Athenas : quod meæ in te observantiæ pignus esse velim. Psalterium a me nuper editum, si forte ad vos usque peruenit, tui, ut spero, recudendi desiderium in te, maximo Ecclesiæ bono, accenderit : quod opus ut acceleres, non tam ego, mihi crede, quam Ecclesia tota efflagitat.[59]

Bèza's own paraphrases were dedicated to the Earl of Huntingdon in a letter dated Geneva, 16 May, 1579. This led David Murray to think that there had been an earlier version of the edition that contained both Buchanan's and Bèze's paraphrases (Morges, 1581), but the letter had already appeared in the separate 1579 edition of Bèze's renderings ; it was reproduced in the joint edition :

> PSALMORVM / SACRORVM DAVIDIS LI- / BRI QVINQVE DUPLICI POE- / tica metaphrasi. altera alteri è regione op- / posita carminum genere Latinè / expressi Theodoro Beza Vezelio, / & Georgio Buchanano Sco- / to autoribus. / Qui rursus, adiunctis quatuordecim Canticis, ex v- / triusque testamenti libris excerptis, argumentis & / Paraphrasi per ipsum Th. Bezam Vezelium illu- / strantur. / EIVSDEM BVCHANANI TRAGOE- / dia quæ inscribitur Iephthes. / Printer's device. / MORGIIS, / Excudebat Ioannes le Preux, Illustriss. Dominorum / Bernensium Typog. / CIↃ.IↃ.LXXXI.
> 8°. 17,75 × 11 cm. A-Z⁸, Aa-Zz⁸, AA-TT⁸, VV². *iv + ** ii + 1042 + 2 blank pp. (not listed in Gardy).
> Copies : A, BM, C, C(Emm. and Tr.), GU(m), NLS, O(W), StA.

Given Bèze's direct links with Buchanan, given too the connection with Vautrollier who had published the Bèze paraphrases in London, there was no reason why this edition should not have Buchanan's blessing, but I have not found proof positive that this was indeed the case. The layout of the paraphrases is as follows : on the *verso* appears the *argumentum* which is continued opposite. Below, *verso*, is the *Paraphrasis* (in italic) followed by Bèze's version (in roman). *Recto* is printed the *Interpretatio* (in roman) followed by Buchanan's paraphrase (in italic). The liminary verse was furnished by Antoine Faye and David Claude. The Buchanan text has taken note of recent alterations, but CV, v. 29 has *strage turbæ* which in

---

[59] *OO*, II, p. 759. The 1580 editions had probably not come out by the time this letter was written.

recent editions had become *strage gentis*, though it must be said that both readings will be found later.

This edition was followed, at some interval, by two other printings from Lepreux who in the meantime had moved to Geneva. The first came out in 1593 (Gardy, No. 236, Copies : A, G, O(StJ)), the second in the following year (Gardy No. 237, Copies : G, O(M)). These editions do not require lengthy description, but they were somewhat enlarged : on the one hand, the *Baptistes* was added to the *Jephthes*, and on the other, the text was not only " emendatior ", but provided with " variis Indicibus, qui Theologiæ candidatis sunt perutiles ", showing that, quite apart from their generally edifying value, the paraphrases were also considered suitable for ordinands. The format of these two editions is smaller than that of the 1581 issue.

The idea of publishing both plays as an accompaniment to the paraphrases may owe something to the example of Jacques Stoer, whose edition had appeared in 1590 :

PARAPHRASIS / PSALMORVM / DAVIDIS POETICA / multò quàm antehac / castigatior ; / *Auctore Georgio Buchanano,* / *Scoto, poëtarum nostri sæculi / facilè principe.* / Adnotata sunt argumenta, & / carminum genera. / *Accesserunt duæ eiusdem BV- / CHANANI Tragœdiæ sacræ* : / *Iephthes seu Votum,* & *Bapti- / stes siue Calumnia.* / TYPIS, / IACOBI STOER, / rule / M.D.XC. The whole title-page has a surrounding frame.

8°. 13 × 7,75 cm. A-Z⁸, Aa⁸-Bb⁴. 196 fol. Main text italic.

Copies : BM, O(N). Reprint, 1591 (Copy : GU(m)).

This edition also includes the original epigram on pilgrimages, the *Canticum Simeonis* of Adolph Metkerk, first printed in Plantin 1582 and henceforth so often reproduced in editions of the paraphrases, and the *Carminum genera.* The letter-preface points out that the Psalm headings will contain references to Bèze's renderings. The volume also contained an epitaph on Buchanan by John Johnston, the Scottish humanist who plays a significant role in the transmission of Buchanan's writings, for it was he who later sent a copy of the *Vita* to Bèze and who was involved in the publication of the *De Sphæra.*

Stoer's edition, I suspect, was a model for the edition produced by Richard Field in London in 1592. This may appear surprising at first blush, for Field was Vautrollier's son-in-law, and one might expect him to follow the lead given by the earlier London editions. However, a short description of his issue will show the resemblance it bears to Stoer's ; incidentally, Stoer who had bought up some of Lepreux' stock for his own edition of the Bèze paraphrases in 1590, may have been encouraged to publish Buchanan's by his knowledge that the two authors were closely connected. Field's edition appears to be fairly rare :

PARAPHRASIS / PSALMORVM / DAVIDIS POETICA / MVLTO QVAM ANTE- / HAC CASTIGATIOR ; / *Auctore Georgio Buchanano, Scoto,* / *poëtarum* / *nostri sæculi facilè principe.* / Adnotata sunt argumenta, & carminum genera. / *Accesserunt duæ eiusdem Buchanani*

Tragœdiœ sacrœ : / *Iephthes seu Votum*, & *Baptistes siue Calumnia*. /
Printer's device / LONDINI / Ex officina typographica Richardi /
Field. 1592
16°. 11,5 × 7 cm. A-Z⁸, Aa-Hh⁸. 4 unnumb. pp. + 5-491 pp. + 1
unnumb. p. with device. Main text italic.
Copies : BM, O.
The volume is very similar to Stoer's by the inclusion of the two tragedies,
the manner in which they are described on the title-page, the references to
the Bèze paraphrases and Johnston's epitaph on Buchanan. Moreover,
Field had intended to include some other works from abroad :

> . . . Ipsius Bezæ quoque paraphrasis cantica Canticorum, nec non
> Ludovici Masurij & aliorum doctissimorum poetarum, in Veteris &
> Noui Testamenti XVII. Cantica sacra metaphrasis poeticæ adiectæ
> sunt.[60]

Nevertheless, Swiss printings, such as those from which Field derived
some of his material, do not increase in number ; it is to Germany that we
must turn to find the most remarkable series of Paraphrase editions, those
initiated by Nathan Chytraeus, of Rostock, in 1585, just about the time
that two Scotsmen, John Johnston, mentioned above, and Robert Howie,
came to spend a year of study there.[61] They studied under the brother of
David Chytraeus, himself a former pupil of Melanchthon and a distinguished
humanist who had created an important centre of Protestant learning, to
which in the fullness of time there came an impressive number of Scotsmen.
Johnston and Howie, among the earliest arrivals, spent a year there before
going their several ways, the former to Helmstädt, the latter to Herborn.
We have few details of their Rostock days, but presumably they met Nathan
Chytræus, who in his early days had studied in Paris, very probably under
Adrien Turnèbe, and who in the early 1580s was engaged upon an edition
of Buchanan's paraphrases, for which he wrote his letter-preface shortly
after the arrival of the young Scots. The first edition appeared in 1585 :

PSALMORVM / DAVIDIS / Paraphrasis poëtica / *GEORGII*
BVCHANANI / *SCOTI* : / *Argumentis explicata*, / *atque illustrata*, /
Opera & studio / *NATHANIS CHYTRAEI*, P.L. / Printer's device
/ *Cum Gratia & Priuileg. Cœs. Maiest.* / FRANCOFORTI / rule /
CIƆ IƆ XCV.
Colophon : FRANCOFORTI MOE- / NVM EXCVDEBAT CHRISTO-
/ PHORVS CORVINVS, ANNO CIƆ IƆ XCV SEPTEMB.
12°. 13 × 7,25 cm. * iv + A-T¹², V⁶. viii + 467 + 1 blank pp.
The *Collectanea* which accompany the Chytraeus editions are separ-
ately paginated and carry their own title-page : viii + 129 pp. + 1
unnumbered page which carries the colophon, giving a more precise
date (iv Sept)
Copies : E, GU, NLS.

---

[60] Or, as is more likely, Field had simply transcribed Stoer's prefatory letter to the
reader and then forgotten its contents ; Field has copied Stoer's preface lock, stock
and barrel.

[61] On these humanists see James K. Cameron, *Letters of John Johnston and Robert
Howie*, St Andrews University Publications No. LIV, Edinburgh and London, 1963.

This edition, like many subsequent ones, was printed by Corvinus, who also brought out the first full edition of the *De Sphœra*.[62] He had begun his printing career in Frankfurt, but various pressures induced him, after he had published the first edition of Chytraeus' edition, to move elsewhere and he settled in Herborn. Here the control of publishing was extremely strict, but Corvinus felt more sympathy with religious attitudes there and he stayed in Herborn for a considerable time ; his 1586 edition of Chytraeus' volume is therefore among the first he published in that town. Herborn was rapidly becoming a centre of Reformation humanism ; its *Gymnasium* had been established in 1584 by Count John VI of Nassau-Dillenburg, it soon began to attract scholars and theologians, and Corvinus was in charge of the press ; in these circumstances one could hardly find a more suitable printing centre for Buchanan's paraphrases.

Chytraeus' edition has several important features. The preface *Lectori candido* sets out the principles underlying his venture. In the first place, he stresses the pedagogic use to which the paraphrases can be put :

> . . . inter alia etiam placuit prudentissimis scholarchis, ut Paraphrasis Psalmorum Buchanani in prima classe proponeretur : ut nimirum ex ea pueri nostri, præter veram pietatem & linguæ Romanæ puritatem, varias etiam carminum, maxime Lyricorum dimensiones animo paulatim comprehenderent.

The religious suitability, though mentioned first, is nevertheless almost taken for granted : Chytraeus appears more concerned with the opportunities these texts afford for a greater familiarity with poetic discourse, Latin idiom and a variety of metrical schemes. Hence his preparation of the *Collectanea* which form a running commentary on the language and style of the paraphrases. In the early editions, over which he had oversight, the *Collectanea* are published with separate pagination, but so popular did they become that in later editions they were taken over, even by publishers in Great Britain, and made to accompany the text.[63] The Psalms are preceded by a brief summary of the themes :

> Primo autem in ea tractatione hoc potissimum egi, ut auditores mei post breue Psalmi cuiuslibet argumentum verba & phrases poëtæ, grammaticè à me explicatas, recto intelligerentur & metaphorarum, aliorumque ornamentorum poëticorum, rationem, rudi, ut aiunt, Minerua expositam utcunque viderent. . .

But Chytraeus went further ; very eager that the paraphrases be provided with their several tunes, he sought the collaboration of a musician from

---

[62] Howie had communicated his copy of the Buchanan manuscript to Johann Pincier who helped him in the preparation of the work for the press (1586). In the following year Pincier provided a more satisfactory edition which also made use of Johnston's manuscript, and also includes Pincier's " completion " of the last two books. On all this see James K. Cameron, op. cit., pp. xxv-xxvii, and James R. Naiden, op. cit., pp. 77 ff.

[63] The Edward Griffin edition of 1648 is based mainly on Chytraeus, including both the *Collectanea* (separately paginated) and the melodies. On the composer responsible for the psalm tunes, see B. Widmann, " Die Kompositionen der Psalmen von Statius Althof ", *Archiv für Musikwissenschaft* V (1889).

46

Osnabruck, Olthoff, who was *primarius cantor* of the Rostock *Gymnasium* : Egi cum primario Scholæ nostræ Cantore, M. Statio Olthovio Osnaburgensi, ut triginta diuersis, quæ in Buchanano continentur, carminum generibus, Melodias certas, partim iam olim ab aliis usurpatas, nonnullas etiam a se ipso modulatas, adiungeret.

These settings, for four voices, were intended not merely to give pleasure, but to be easily learned by the pupils. Chytraeus wanted the boys to know the psalms by heart : music would surely be a help in this direction, and the boys would be able to sing them at various times of the day :

> Vade etiam illud est consecutum, ut singulis horis, sub initia & finem exercitiorum scholasticorum, primani nostri ipsi inter se Psalmum aliquem quatuor vocibus, sine notis, quas vocant, Musicis canendo, aliquoties totum Psalterium iam absoluerit : atque ita (quod mihi certè audita iucundissimum est laudibus & celebrationibus hominis diuini multoties quotidie repetitis locus gymnasio & domicilio nostro assignatus undique resonet.

Under these circumstances, Buchanan's paraphrases could cover a very wide pedagogic range, creating proper religious attitudes, enriching the pupils' latinity, furthering musical experience, and Chytraeus towards the end of the preface sums up the value of the edition, as he sees it :

> . . . ut . . . atque ita aliis quoque non solum exercitiorum veræ pietatis & Musicæ religiosæ, verum etiam linguæ naturæ plenius intelligendæ hoc modo præberetur occasio.

There was another valuable feature : the edition contained the first biographical sketch of Buchanan to be printed. The *Vita ab ipso scripta* was not published until 1598 by the antiquarian J. J. Boissard, and, once again, Johnston was involved, for he sent a copy to Bèze in 1595.[64] However, there is no indication that he possessed the text as early as his Rostock days, and Chytraeus contented himself with putting together, not always accurately, such autobiographical references as he had been able to glean from Buchanan's works published till that time. His narrative tends to stress the pedagogic and religious aspects of the Scotsman's career, but he did obtain some details at first-hand from Scotsmen resident in Rostock :

> Interea tamen ex Scotis quibusdam cognoui, paraphrasten cognomen hoc non tam a patria, quam a parentibus & maioribus suis gentilitium accepisse.

It is tempting to think that Johnston and Howie may have given some help to Chytraeus, who also narrates at length an episode in Buchanan's tutorship of King James VI, but this information came to him by another channel (through his friend Iacobus Monauius back to Andreas Dudith, Ioannes

---

[64] The *Vita* was first printed in the *Icones quinquaginta virorum illustrium* . . . *cum eorum vitis descriptis* à I. I. Boissardo, Franfort, T. de Bry, 4 parts, 1597-9. Parts 1 and 2 were undertaken by Boissard, the other two by J. A. Lonicer. The *Vita* is printed in pt. 3, pp. 23-32. It was published again in 1608 at Frankfort, separately, and in the same year another printing appeared without indication of place. As Professor James K. Cameron points out, op. cit., p. 107, a letter of John Johnston removes the doubts once entertained about the authenticity of this text. Chytraeus' sketch, *De Paraphraste ipso Georgio Buchanano*, precedes the *Collectanea*.

Metellus Sequanus and ultimately Buchanan's nephew). Chytraeus' sketch naturally lost its point once the *Vita* was printed and it vanished in due course from later editions.

The Chytraeus edition was immensely successful, and not merely because it was printed in great measure for the captive audience of a *Gymnasium*, for it was freely exploited by later editors right down to the XVIIIth century : indeed, one of the best critical editions, prepared by Robert Hunter and John Love and published in Edinburgh (1737), made considerable use of Chytraeus in addition to the work of later scholars. In addition to the two issues mentioned by David Murray, but not yet seen by myself, I have come across the following editions which bear eloquent witness to the popularity of Chytraeus' industry :

1586 (mentioned by Murray, op. cit., p. 422)
1588 BM
1590 G, GU, O(Q). The type has been reset and there are minor differences of type and line-setting
1592 BM
1595 BM, GU(m), StA
1600 BM, NLS, O, StA
1608 StA
1610 C, GU(m)
1613 GU(m), NLS. In this edition, the Chytraeus biographical sketch is replaced by the *Vita*
1616 G(Tc), GU, O
1619 StA
1624 BM, C, GU(m), L. O
1637 D, GU(m), StA
1646 StA
1656 StA
1664 BM, StA
1703 (mentioned by David Murray, op. cit., p. 423).

Further editions may come to light in due course ; and yet, there were some other printings in Germany during this period. One or two of these may be connected one way or another with the Chytraeus edition : thus, the one printed in Siegen in 1597 (Copies : GU, NLS) is explained by the fact that Corvin had moved there and simply made use of the Herborn formula ; and the 1619 Bremen edition (Copy : C), which also has the musical settings and was printed for use in the local school, may be connected with the fact that Chytraeus had become Principal there before he died in 1592. There is a small, separate current of German editions : Cologne, 1586 (Copy : GU(m)), Wittemberg, 1595 (Copy : NLS) and Wittemberg, 1597 (Copy : GU(m)). These are all connected : they give the bare text, with simply the liminary poem to Mary Queen of Scots and an indication of the *carminum genera* under each Psalm heading ; there are no musical settings, no separate section on the metres, no commentary on grammatical points. The Cologne edition has been followed by the two Wittemberg issues, though there has been reprinting in each case and there are minor variations of printing

48

conventions. Psalm I has the older reading *celeri ludibria vento*, in the
Cologne edition ; the others claim that their text is " multo quam antehac
castigatior ".[65]

The history of the German editions of the Paraphrases is therefore
essentially that of the Chytraeus formula. In France, there continues to be
little interest in Buchanan's versions, though one edition is worth noting,
that brought out at Chalons in 1601 : this volume, which also contained the
two Latin plays, was destined for a Catholic public :

> PARAPHRASIS / PSALMORVM / DAVIDIS POETICA. / *Authore*
> GEORGIO BVCHANANO, / *Scoto, Poëtarum nostri sœculi / facilè
> principe.* / Addita sunt piæ precationes singulæ singulis Psalmis
> respondentes. / ITEM, / *Accessere Tragœdiæ eiusdem Authoris quarum
> / prima Iephthes seu votum, altera Baptistes / siue calomnia inscribitur.*
> / CATHALAVNI. / Apud CLAVDIVM GVYOT, / Typograph Reg-
> ium. / rule. / 1601.
> 12°. 12 × 6,5 cm. Title-sheet, A-O¹² + A-D¹² + E⁶. xx + 333 pp.
> + 1 unnumb. p. + 54 fol. (no pagination). The printing conventions
> are not used systematically throughout. The *Oratio* to Psalm XXII
> (p. 47) opens : Deus, qui es laus & gloria Ecelsiæ (sic) Catholicæ pro
> nobis opprobrium factus in ligno crucis. . . .
> Copies : BM, BN, GU(m).

This edition is interesting solely for the attempt made to use Buchanan's
paraphrases to Catholic ends ; this is not an isolated example in France, for
we shall find another example on a more limited scale in the XVIIIth century.

So far, neither England nor Scotland have cut a very impressive figure
in the spread of Buchanan's work : Richard Field's work was sadly derivative
and only his father-in-law had made a positive contribution (Vautrollier,
1580 and 1583). In the second decade of the XVIIth century, however,
there is a little flurry of activity, though we shall have to wait a bit longer
before British editions really get under way. The first Scottish edition appears
in 1611 from the press of Andrew Hart of Edinburgh :

> PARAPHRASIS / PSALMORVM / DAVIDIS / POETICA. / *Auctore*
> / Georgio Buchanano, / *Scoto, poëtarum nostri* / seculi facilè / principe.
> / rule / Adnotata vbique diligenter carminum genera. /rule / *Acces-
> serunt duae ejusdem* Buchanani / *Tragœdiæ sacrae : Iephthes, seu
> Vo-* / *tum &* Baptistes *sive Calumnia.* / Pattern and rule / *EDIN-*

[65] There is one other German edition which appears as it were in isolation :
PARAPHRASIS / PSALMO- / RVM DAVIDIS POETICA, PRIORIBVS /
editionibus antehac multò castigatior : / *CVM BREVISSIMIS ARGV- /
mentis cuiuslibet Psalmi Dn. Nicodemi Frischlini* / P.L. & C.P. *antea nusquam
visis.* / AVCTORE / GEORGIO BVCHANANO SCOTO / Poëtarum nostri
sæculi facilè principe. / *Adnotata vbique diligenter carminum genera.* / Accessit
demum INDEX Psalmorum secun- / dum Alphabeti ordinem : / Printer's device
/FRANCOFVRTI, / Ex officina MATTHIÆ BECKERI. / rule / *M.D.CV.* /
rule
12°. 15 × 9 cm. A-R⁸. 267 + 5 unnumb. pp. Main text roman.
Copies : A, GU.
This edition is not very carefully printed, but it shows some original features : Frisch-
lin's summaries and the alphabetical index. There are no musical settings. A fair
number of editions of Buchanan's other writings, especially the *Historia* and the *De
Jure regni*, are printed in Frankfort.

BURGI. / *Excudebat* Andreas Hart, / Bibliopôla. / The title is within a rectangular surround : at the top centre is inserted Andreas / Hart, and at the bottom Anno 1611.
8°. 12 × 7,5 cm. A-V⁸. No pagination. Main text roman. The volume contains the *Canticum Simeonis* of A. Metkerk.
Copies : BM, StA.
This edition, with the inclusion of the two tragedies, described as *sacræ*, reminds one of certain continental issues, and Hart of course had close connections abroad, in particular with Frankfurt. Another issue of the 1611 volume came out, also at Edinburgh, in 1621 (Copy : BM). More important in certain respects, was the edition he brought out in 1615 :

GEORGII / BVCHANANI / SCOTI, / *POEMATA* / omnia innumeris penè / *locis, ex ipsius autographo* / castigata & aucta. / ADDITO INSVPER / ex eodem, Miscellaneorum / *libro, nunc primùm in* / lucem edito. / Printer's device / *EDINBVRGI,* / Ex officina ANDREÆ HART, / *ANNO* 1615.
24°. 11 × 5,75 cm. * ⁸, A-M¹², A-L¹², M⁶. No pagination. Main text roman.[66]
Copies : BM, C, NLS, O(N).

The Paraphrases are printed in the first section (A 1ʳ-I7ʳ) and are followed by the *Hymnus Matutinus* and the *Canticum Simeonis* ; the section concludes with the two Latin plays. The edition was important on two counts : on the one hand, the " profane " poems had undoubtedly been printed with the help of a manuscript source, but it is not so clear that the paraphrases, which contain a number of misprints, also benefited from sources hitherto untapped. And on the other hand, this Hart edition was the first to publish together the sacred and the profane poems, a pattern that will be followed frequently, and in particular abroad. Indeed, David Murray and Maitland Anderson both expressed the view that the volume could well have been produced in Amsterdam or Leyden :

The 1615 edition, as issued along with Buchanan's poetical works, may have been printed in Edinburgh, but it has all the appearance of having been imported from Holland.[67]

A man who played an important part in the production of the 1615 edition was John Ray, an Edinburgh schoolmaster ; and his name appears among the authors of liminary verse for another edition which, though published in London, was the work of a Scots colleague :

ECPHRASIS / PARAPHRASEOS / *Georgij Buchanani* in Psalmos / DAVIDIS : Ab ALEXANDRO IVLIO / *EDINBURGENO,* / In Adolescentiæ studiosæ / gratiam elaborata. / rule / Printer's device / rule / LONDINI, / Excusum apud Georgium Eld, / M.DC.XX.
8°. A-Z⁸, Aa⁸. xvi + 364 + 4 blank pp. Main text italic, marginal commentary roman.
Copies : C, GU(m), NLS, StA, O.
A further edition brought out by J. Vallange, Edinburgh, in 1699.
Copies : A, BM, GU(m), O, StA, StA(hf).

---

[66] For a more detailed description see my previously mentioned article in *The Library*, p. 330.
[67] Maitland Anderson, op. cit., p. 11.

This edition was not only reprinted in its own right, but its commentary was exploited by later editors for pedagogic purposes. The special interest of the book was that the commentary went back in part to Buchanan himself. Alexander Yule, in his youth, had made bold to consult the author himself and later, when he was teaching at Stirling and using the paraphrases as a textbook, he thought it worth while to provide a commentary for a wider spectrum of schoolchildren :

> Iecit ergo *Georgius* ille *Buchananus* primum operis hujus fundamentum, materiamque rudem & impolitam magnâ ex parte suffecit. Unde hæc structuræ forma elementer & molliter assurrexit, in qua ne unguem quidem latum ab ejus mente & sententiâ discedere fas esse judicavi, quem in toto hoc opere præcipuum auctorem & grauem veræ exegesis testem habere, ab omnibus bene de re literaria sentientibus probatum fore, mihi minime dubitandum est. (f. A 3r-r)

Buchanan's authority was therefore a significant factor in the success of Yule's commentary ; but it is curious to think that, whereas in his own time, the paraphrase was considered to be an aid towards the understanding of a difficult Hebrew text, his composition should come to require its own commentary.

These various editions of the years 1611-20 are, however, not immediately followed up in Great Britain ; before we see the development of a steady stream of editions at home, we must once again see what was going on abroad. From now on, activity is confined almost exclusively to Holland, and in two ways. First of all, there are the Elzevier editions of the Paraphrases. Budik and David Murray both make reference to an edition brought out by H. Laurents in 1618, but I have not seen a copy and Goldsmid makes no mention of it either.[68] On the other hand, the 1621 edition, " ex typis Isaaci Elzevir ", is known ; it also contains the two Latin plays, and though it is described by Goldsmid as " extremely rare ", it is preserved in several libraries (C, E, St A). This edition is followed by a few others :

> 1628   Described by Goldsmid, I, p. 54 ; I have not seen a copy ;
> 1650   This edition contains several of the misprints found in 1621, but Jansson has omitted the traditional poem to Mary Queen of Scots. (Copies : BM, C, StA (hf)) ;
> 1688   Mentioned, without location, by D. Murray, op. cit., p. 423.[69]

In the second place, the Hart edition of 1615 set an example that was followed especially on the continent and, indeed, apart from the Saumur edition, always in Amsterdam or Leyden. These editions of the *Poemata omnia* begin with the Saumur edition of 1620-1 :

> GEORGII BVCHANANI /SCOTI / *POETARUM SVI SÆCVLI* / *facilè principis poëmata quæ super-* / *sunt omnia, in tres partes diuisa* / *multò quàm antehac* / emendatiora. / CATALOGVM EORVM QVÆ / hac editione continentur 3 exhibebit pagella. / Printer's device /

---

[68] E. Goldsmid, *A Complete Catalogue of all the Elzevier Presses.* . . Edinburgh, 3 vols. 1885-8, vol. I, p. 54.

[69] Edinburgh University Library, however, possesses an edition by H. Laurentz, without date or place of publication.

SALMVRII, / Sumpt. CL. GIRARDI / DAN. LERPINERII. /
IOAN. BURELLI / *ANNO M.DC.XXI.*
Copies : A, BN, StA, V.

The edition is in two volumes and a detailed description would be out of
place here.[70] The paraphrases occupy pp. 15-226 of the first volume and
are followed by the *Hymnus matutinus,* the *Canticum Simeonis* and the two
Latin plays. The second volume, containing the profane poems, is in fact
dated 1620, though the section containing the *De Sphœra* has a separate
title-page bearing the date 1621 ; there follow the translations of the *Medea*
and the *Alcestis.* The appearance of this edition is explained by the fact
that Saumur was then a centre of Calvinist activity with its own academy.
It numbered on its staff many distinguished Scotsman, and indeed its first
rector was John Glasford. Two later Principals of Glasgow University
taught there : Robert Boyd and John Cameron ; and William Craig was
professor of philosophy there from 1601 to 1616. The Saumur edition sought
to improve upon the Hart 1615 by incorporating the *Medea* and the *Alcestis,*
so that it could reasonably claim to be the most complete edition of Buchanan's poetical works so far published ; but it also offered a text of the *De
Sphœra* corrected from a manuscript which had passed from John Geddy
" servitor to Mr. George Buchquhannan " to his brother William who was
then teaching at Saumur. Moreover, it contained notes and variants, and
it has been thought that this editorial work was undertaken by John
Cameron.[71] Nevertheless, some mystery surrounds this edition, and three
hypotheses have been advanced : (i) the Saumur edition is based upon an
Elzevier edition of 1620, now lost but also the source of Elzevier 1621 ;
(ii) Elzevier 1621, whose pagination is the same as Saumur, is really the
1620 one which, though used for Saumur before publication, did not in fact
appear until the following year ; (iii) Elzevier 1621 is based on the Saumur
edition. The matter is still far from clear, but one must assume that the
idea of publishing this edition started in Saumur, since certain source-
material derives from Scotsmen on the staff there.[72]

Whatever the truth of the matter, a series of *Poemata omnia,* with a
variable inclusion of the plays, come into being. With the exception of the
great Ruddiman editions that close the sequence, they do not add anything
that is textually significant ; but they do give us some idea of Buchanan's
continuing popularity. I give a summary list, including one or two mentioned
by other bibliographers :

1624   Saumur, reprint of Elzevier 1621. (Copy : Amst)
1628   Two Elzevier editions (Leyden) :

[70] James R. Naiden, op. cit., pp. 160-1, describes this edition in some detail ; he
has found further copies in the Bibliothèque Municipale, Bordeaux and at the University of Marburg.

[71] See D. Murray, op. cit., pp. 481-2 and James R. Naiden, op. cit., p. 161.

[72] For description of the Elzevier 1621, see E. Goldsmid, op. cit., I, p. 55. Copies :
BN, D, NLS.

(i) 8°. 511 pp. (Copy : BN)
(ii) 24°. 561 pp. (Copy : BN)

1641   Amsterdam, Janssonius. 24°. 561 pp. (reprint of 1628) (Copies : BM, BN, D, GU, NLS, StA)

1647   Amsterdam, mentioned by L. Bradner, *Musæ anglicanæ*, p. 353

1657   Amsterdam, Wetstein, mentioned by D. Murray, op. cit., p. 484, but perhaps a misprint for 1687

1665   Amsterdam, J. Waesberge & E. Weyerstraet. 24°. 529 + 14 unnumb. + 2 blank pp. (Copies : BM, C, GU, NLS, O, O(Q), V)

1676   Amsterdam, D. Elsevir. 24°. 531 + 10 unnumb. + 3 blank pp. (Copies : A, BM, BN, D, GU, L, NLS, O, StA)

1677   Edinburgh, John Cairns. *Poemata quæ supersunt*. 12°. 705 pp. Appears to be a bulky reprint of Amsterdam 1665. There is another Edinburgh printing (*Poemata postrema*, Copy : BM). Copies of the first issue are more frequent : A, BM, GU, NLS.

1680   J. R. Naiden, op. cit., p. 165, mentions the reported sale of an Elzevier 1680 by *Bottega d'Erasmo* in 1949

1686   London, B. Griffin. Conflates material from the Dutch and Chytraeus editions. 610 pp. (Copies : A, Br, C, D, E, L, NLS, O(A), StA)

1687   Amsterdam, H.Wetstein. There are two slightly different issues of this edition ; I have compared the two in C (*a* = kkk.748 ; *b* = kkk.747) : *a* has its 546 pp. with p. 546 properly paginated, but p. 345 wrongly numbered as p. 346 ; on the title-page POËMATIA has a trema. The C copy has gathering Q (pp. 241-56) incorrectly inserted between pp. 272-3. Copy *b* has p. 546 wrongly numbered as 549, has no trema on the title-page. The two issues differ slightly in the type and in details of the portrait. (Copies of both issues in the following libraries : A, BM, C)

1715   The famous Ruddiman, Edinburgh, edition in two volumes, of the *Opera omnia*. (Copies : A, E, C, O, etc. ; very common)

1716   London, R. Gosling. Appears to be a reissue of Griffin, 1686. (Copies : BM, C, StA)

1725   The Ruddiman-Burmann edition of the *Opera Omnia*, Leyden, 2 volumes. (Copies are very common)

Towards the end of this list we gain a hint of the way things are developing : foreign editions will make way for a greater number at home. Indeed, during the XVIIIth century, though Buchanan's reputation as a " profane " poet will remain firmly established, the paraphrases no longer command the same public. David Murray refers to one Swiss edition of 1721 ;[73] and in France, where there had been one selection of psalms published in the XVIIth century, after the Chalons issue,[74] very much the same pattern

---

[73] Published at Basel, mentioned, without location, by D. Murray, op. cit., p. 423. There is a German edition published at Stendal, 1710 (Copy : GU).

[74] Le P. Labbé had included Buchanan in his *Heroicæ poeseos deliciæ ad unius Virgilii imitationem*, Paris, 1646. Ruddiman, *OO*, I, fol. 1 viii^v -m, has assembled some tributes to Buchanan by French men of letters active during the XVIIth century. One might add that the Pontus de Thyard Library (containing books belonging to Pontus I and Pontus II) possessed a copy of the Paraphrases.

occurs in the following century ; in 1729 a curious volume appeared, dedicated to the French king :

NOVA ET ACCURATA / EDITIO PSALMORVM / DAVIDIS, / UNÀ CUM PARAPHRASI / BUCHANANI / POËTAE CELE- / BERRIMI. / *Opus Regi dedicatum.* / PARS PRIMA. / Printer's device / PARISIIS, / Apud CLAUDIUM DE HANSY, Bibliopolam / in Ponte qui vulgò dicitur, le Pont au / Change, sub insigne S. Claudii. / rule / M.DCC.XXIX. / *Cum Approbatione & Privilegio Regis.* cxxx + 504 pp. + Pars secunda which has similar title-page, 206 pp. Copy : BN.

The author, De L'Estang, was trying to repeat one of the aims we noted in the Renaissance, the use of paraphrase to help understanding of texts that were far from clear, but he also sought elegant latinity. He hoped that his edition of Buchanan's paraphrases, printed out of their normal order (with the Vulgate opposite) to suit the office would meet with the approval of the clergy, but also " des Princes, des Magistrats, & des grands de tous les ordres du Royaume qui assistent à l'Office Divin " (I, p. vii). In his Latin *Præfatio* he commends the metrical variety of Buchanan's paraphrases and makes some interesting comparisons with those of Jean de Gagny and Théodore de Bèze :

> Versio Ganei diffusior est, & prosam nimium sapit. Bezæ vero stylus durior est & turgidior locutionibus nimium figuratis & perplexis scatens.[75]

This venture, and the publication, nearly a hundred years later, of J. B. Rousseau's renderings of seventeen Buchanan paraphrases,[76] mark the end of a literary reputation that was after all never very thriving in France.

In England, one cannot speak of high success either, but there are a number of Griffin editions during the Commonwealth or thereabouts—this is a period when Buchanan's political writings enjoy some success—and a few also appear during the XVIIIth century. The Griffin editions were much dependent on foreign printings :

1640   London, Edward Griffin. (Copies : BM, C)
1648   London, Edward Griffin. (Copies : A, G(Tc), StA, StA(hf))
1648   London, Sarah Griffin. (Copies : BM, GU(m))
1660   London, Sarah Griffin. There are two different issues, both derived from the 1648 edition. StA has copies of both (A : Buch BS 1442, B8C60B ; B : Buch BS 1442, B8C60). Both differ slightly in their print, and though each carries the same material on the page, the disposition, especially in the *argumenta*, is usually a shade different.
   A keeps Edward Griffin's device, the flaming heart, whereas B introduces the fleur-de-lys. In A FINIS on p. 478 is in roman in B, in italic. Most important, whereas in A the *Collectanea* are dated 1660 (as one would expect), in B they

---

[75] Op. cit., p. lxi ; on pp. lxii-lxv, textual comparisons are provided between the three authors.

[76] In his *Œuvres choisies*, published in 1818. Buchanan's profane poems, on the other hand, were known and respected for a very long time in France.

carry the date 1572 (p. 377), which, taken with the change of
device, suggests that we are dealing with a later edition.[77]

1683 London. (Copy : BM)

1742 London, with Psalm paraphrases in Greek by James Duport,
Master of Magdalene College. (Copies : A, GU(m), O)

1775 London, D. Goodsman. (Copies : BM, StA.)

The other current is the exceptional number of editions that are published
in Scotland. In the XVIIth century, the Hart editions (1611, 1615, 1621)
had not provided the impetus that one might have expected, but in the
following century, the stream becomes a river : not only do editions pro-
liferate, but critical commentaries are often added, and in the early part of
the XIXth century, these commentaries may be supplemented by English
translations. Scotland may have been somewhat tardy in recognising the
pedagogic value of Buchanan's psalms, but once they became part of the
curriculum, they took deep root. Nonetheless, the humanist's supremacy
was not always unchallenged. In the early 1600s, Thomas Eglisham, phys-
ician to James VI, had tried to assert his own superiority over Buchanan,
and though he was laughed out of court, one cannot say that the paraphrases
were all that successful in Scotland during the first half of the century,
after the Hart printings.[78] Some hundred years later, another dispute arose :
on this occasion the paraphrases were compared unfavourably with those of
Arthur Jonston, but stoutly defended by Ruddiman. Some perhaps had
not forgotten that Buchanan had written poems of a very different flavour,
and in any case many were still preoccupied with the problems raised by
the use of a pagan idiom in a religious context.[79] For a variety of reasons,
Buchanan took longer to establish himself as a poet in his own native land,
the last to print editions of both the profane and sacred poems. Here space
allows for only the briefest of lists to show the popularity of the paraphrases
after the middle of the XVIIth century, but as before I shall note a few
editions which, not yet seen by myself, are mentioned by serious critics :

1660 Edinburgh, Gid. Lithgo (together with the two Latin plays).
Mentioned by Budik

1672 Aberdeen, J. Forbes. Mentioned sceptically by Maitland
Anderson (op. cit., p. 11), it is in fact listed by Wing (two
copies) ; and this may well be the 1672 edition mentioned in
the Catalogue of the Bibl. Lindesiana

1684 Glasgow, Sanders (Copy : GU(m))

1694 Edinburgh, Mosman (mentioned by D. Murray under Norman,
op. cit., p. 423, and also by Budik)

---

[77] Wing does not differentiate between the two editions in the copies he lists (FSF,
O, TU, Y).

[78] D. Irving, op. cit., p. 128 ; D. Murray, op. cit., pp. 426-7.

[79] D. Irving, op. cit., pp. 124 ff. ; A. Menzies, " Buchanan's Psalms : an Eighteenth-
century Controversy ", *George Buchanan : A Memorial*, St Andrews, 1907, pp. 136-
42 ; D. Duncan, *Thomas Ruddiman*, Edinburgh and London, 1965, pp. 116 ff. On
Ruddiman's edition of Buchanan's *Opera omnia*, see also D. Duncan, op. cit., pp. 62 ff.
(with special reference to the Psalm paraphrases, p. 62).

1695 Reprint of previous edition, mentioned by D. Murray.
1699 New edition of A. Yule's *Ecphrasis* (see above, p. 49)
1716 Edinburgh, Freebairn : 1st Ruddiman edition (Copies : GU(m),
      NLS, StA)
1725 Edinburgh, William Adam : 2nd Ruddiman edition, with notes
      by himself, Chytraeus and Julius. (Copies : A, BN, O, StA)
1730 Edinburgh, Thomas Heriot, 3rd, improved Ruddiman edition.
      (Copy : StA)
1732 Edinburgh, Freebairn, Ruddiman edition. (Copy : GU(m))
1737 Edinburgh, T. & W. Ruddiman. Edited by Robert Hunter
      and John Love. (Copies : A, BM, BN, E, GU(m), NLS, O,
      StA)
1750 Glasgow, Robert Urie. No commentary, but finely printed.
      (Copies : A, BM, BN, C, D, GM, GU(m), O, StA)
1762 Edinburgh, A. Kincaid & J. Bell. Includes the two Latin
      plays. (Copy : NLS)
1764 A similar edition to 1762, mentioned by D. Murray, op. cit.,
      p. 420
1765 Glasgow, R. & A. Foulis. (Copies : BM, GU(m), O, StA)
1772 Edinburgh, J. Robertson. Contains the plays with Andrew
      Waddel's translation " into English prose ". Waddel had a
      school in the Canongate and his version was frequently re-
      printed. (Copies : BM, GU(m), O)
1775 London, Alexander Grant. Waddel's edition. (Copies : BM,
      StA)
1786 Edinburgh, J. Dickson & W. Creech. Waddel's edition.
      (Copies : B, BM)
1790 Glasgow, J. Gillies. Contains Ruddiman's notes. (Copies :
      E, StA)
1793 Edinburgh. Another edition with Ruddiman's notes. (Copies :
      BM, L, StA)
1797 Glasgow, J. Mundell, and Edinburgh, J. Dickson, J. Fair-
      bairn, A. Constable. Ruddiman's edition. (Copy : StA)
1807 Edinburgh, C. Stewart. Listed by D. Murray, op. cit., p. 421
1812 Edinburgh (Typ. Acad,). Notes by Adam Dickinson. (Copy :
      GU)
1815 Edinburgh, J. Pillans ; based on the 1797 edition. (Copies :
      O, StA)
1815 (?) Glasgow. Title-page missing. (Copy : GU(m))
1825 Edinburgh (Typ. Acad.). Further issue of Ruddiman edition.
      (Copies : BM, GU(m))

There are several other translations of the Psalms into English : that by
the Rev. Thomas Cradock, printed at Wells in 1754, may conceivably have
reached an American audience, as the translator was a minister in Mary-
land ; James Fanch translated a selection in 1764 (London) and John Eadie
rendered the paraphrases into English verse in 1836. There are also versions
of individual psalms that may be found scattered in periodicals. These
latter translations were probably in the nature of literary exercises, but the
main success of Buchanan's psalms lay in the value they had for the grammar school curriculum, and there they hold a privileged place for some
hundred and fifty years.

Though we have followed the fortunes of the paraphrases through the centuries, we have not considered closely enough the reasons that originally prompted Buchanan to compose them. They may have helped him to while away the time when he was confined to his Portuguese monastery, but we have seen that the psalm paraphrase was popular in France well before Buchanan left for Portugal, and also that he took the trouble, many years later, to complete them and furthermore to revise them. By looking a little more closely at this problem, I hope that we shall dispel two currently held views about Psalm paraphrases in the sixteenth century : on the one hand that they were essentially literary pastimes,[80] and on the other that " of course these translations were not based on the original Hebrew or Greek texts, but on the Latin prose of the Vulgate ".[81] Though no doubt humanists could be expected to take pleasure in the literary excellence of their Latin writing, whether in verse or in prose, one must remember that, first, eloquence was connected in the humanist mind with moral progress, and second, that in a period of high religious strife and ferment, it would be difficult for a genre like the psalm paraphrase to remain a literary matter. It is true that Latin paraphrase of the psalm went beyond sectarian boundaries ; it is also true that the views of Catholic and Reformed paraphrasts overlapped in certain respects ; but the religious colour of the age would make it difficult for an evangelical humanist, still less a convinced Reformer, to be satisfied with the Vulgate version. Let us, however, first look at the ideas voiced by Jean de Gagnay ; his attitude is surely orthodox, but he does express points that could very properly be shared by Buchanan, who we have already seen was associated with Gagnay before he left for Portugal.

In the Preface Gagnay draws attention to the range of human appeal held by the Psalms, which more than other Biblical texts, are constantly on the lips of the priest :

> Nullus enim sacrorum librorum est, in quo tot hominum genera contineantur. . . Itaque cum tam necessarium atque utilem esse Christianis librum maiores nostri intelligerent, probi constituerunt ut in diuinis officiis psalmi decantarentur.[82]

Indeed, it is because of this last factor that a proper understanding of the Psalms is so important ; Gagnay stresses the need for intelligibility more than the lyrical qualities possessed by the Psalms, and in this he takes the same line as Marcantonio Flaminio ; both are agreed that these texts present considerable problems of interpretation, and in this context the value of reliable paraphrase is obvious :

> Hinc factum, ut nullus liber frequentius labiis Christianorum tenatur & sacerdotum maxime : atque non labiis modo, ut verè possent cum Paulo dicere, psallam spiritu, psallam & mente . . . nullus est inter sacros libros difficilior, siue propter hebraismos à septuaginta interpre-

---

[80] J. A. Gaertner, art. cit., passim.
[81] W. Leonard Grant, art. cit., p. 205, note 1.
[82] J. Gagnaeus, op. cit., fol. * ii^r.

tibus (à quibus sumpta est ecclesiastica versio) no perspicuè redditos, siue propter ἀναπόδοτα in psalmis frequentia, seu propter latentis prophetiæ obscuritatem. . . .

Intelligibility is therefore the first concern, but since one may always combine *dulce* with *utile*, the use of verse in the paraphrase may be adjuvant :

> Itaque genus aliquod tractandorum psalmorum (quod ad eorum lectionem pios homines inuitaret) meditanti mihi nullum occurrebat commodius, quam si carmine tractarentur : quod id genus vi quadam & dicendi gratia allicere lectores soleat.

But one must go further : it is not sufficient to render the psalms into, say, elegiac couplets ; the variety of mood and theme must be matched by a corresponding diversity of metre. Gagnay takes exception to writers who fail to recognise the force of this point :

> Quanquam vero non ignorabam a tribus ante me in metrorum ordinem ac rationem coactos esse psalmos, Germanis duobus & uno Gallo : non tamen decedendum mihi duxi a proposita semel sententia : quod qui ante me id oneris aggressi essent, uno eodemque metri genere psalmos perscripsissent, elegiaco scilicet, quod genus lugubribus primum & miserabilibus querimoniis iuxta vocabuli ἔτυμον accommodatum est : deinde vero ad amatoria transijt. Longe diuertissima sunt autem in psalmis argumentorum genera : . . . Itaque cum iudicarem non omni pedi omnem calceum aptum esse, existimabam quoque non uno carminis genere tot tamque diuersa psalmorum argumenta commode tractari posse : multoque fore commodius, si varijs odarum generibus describerentur... Ausus itaque sum, deo bene iuuante, in varia odarum genera psalmos transfundere, quod nemo, opinor, ante me tentauerat. Nam præter elegiacos illos poetas, perpaucos lyricis versibus psalmos Germani aliquot ediderant.

Finally, Gagnay approaches the problem of using a pagan idiom to express a Christian theme ; he does not find this so thorny a matter as did some later critics of Buchanan. He follows Prudentius in the quantities adopted for Hebrew words, and makes a few suggestions for the handling of vocabulary :

> Hoc autem admonitum lectorem volumus, non usque adeo verborum puritati nos studuisse, ut recepta in ecclesiam vocabula (quorum neque rem neque nomen Ciceronis ætas nouerat) abiiceremus, ac pro illis noua cudere laboraremus : qualia sunt fides pro religione, fidelis pro religioso . . .

In this preface, therefore, Gagnay covers a variety of matters that were bound to concern the budding paraphrast ; he gives a religious justification for the exercise and he also shows how stylistic and metrical considerations can be properly introduced to this end. He does not, on the other hand, say much about the way in which one should try to tackle the problem of intelligibility ; indeed, he skirts the difficult question of the linguistic study of the texts. Nevertheless, this was a most important issue in that age of religious controversy and frequently debated in the *milieux* where the influence of Erasmus and evangelical humanism continued to make itself felt. And this raises the whole question of Buchanan's sources.

Historically speaking, the discussion of these sources has centred more particularly on Buchanan's debt to the classics. Irving reminds us of certain borrowings from the Golden Age : thus the opening line of IV is taken bodily from *Aeneid*, X, 18, with the one change of *rerumque* to *diuumque* :

O pater, o hominum diuumque æterna potestas

and LXXXII, v. 1, opens with two lines hardly bothering to disguise their Horatian origin :

Regum timendorum in proprios greges,
Reges in ipsos imperium est Jouae.[83]

One could add that in certain psalms, such as XXIV, the passages describing Nature are substantially amplified by recourse to classical models. In Psalm CIV, often considered the height of his achievement, Buchanan introduces many a classical echo ; for instance in v. 8 :

. . . . paullatim ascendere montes
Cernere erat, sensimque cauas subsidere valles. . .

cauas valles is surely a reminiscence of *Georgics*, II, 390, while the antithesis at the line-ends of *ascendere montes . . . subsidere valles* recalls a similar contrast in *Metamorphoses*, I, 43-4 (*subsidere valles . . . surgere montes*). And one would have no difficulty in multiplying examples to prove Buchanan's dependence on classical models. But all this hides his relationship to his own times in the way he has tackled the problems of paraphrase. He is very close to Gagnay in the creation of a correspondence between the mood of a psalm and its metrical form ; and he also has devoted a very great deal of thought to problems of intelligibility and a proper expression of the real meaning of the Biblical text. Here, I think that Buchanan with his evangelical leanings goes further than Gagnay, and does not content himself with a paraphrase of the Vulgate, though of course he uses it from time to time. Let us try to find out how Buchanan set about his task.

In the first place, it has been recognised for a long time that Buchanan moved in circles where Hebrew scholarship was genuine and serious. William Barclay, who defended Buchanan against Eglisham's pretentions, wrote :

Doctissimus poeta sequutus Francisci Vatabli psalmorum interpretationem ; quem Parisiis Hebraicæ linguæ professorem habuit summe amicum et familiarem. Itaque consulebat curiose fontes ipsos, et linguam qua psalmos cecinit *regius propheta*. Unde deducit aliquando plus sententiæ quam appareat in vulgatis editionibus.[84]

There is nothing more likely than that Buchanan, for so long in the French capital, where he both studied and taught, knew Vatable well ; but Barclay was writing long after Buchanan's death and I have not so far found contemporary, first-hand evidence to support his remarks. If there is substance in

[83] D. Irving, op. cit., pp. 126-7. Le. P. Labbé, it will be remembered, had in the XVIIth century chosen paraphrases by Buchanan that were strongly Vergilian in flavour.

[84] *Iudicium de certamine G. Eglisemmii cum G. Buchanano*, London, 1620, p. 14, quoted by D. Irving, op. cit., p. 125. Robert Estienne published the so-called *Biblia Vatabli* in 1545.

this, one will have to accept also that Buchanan's interest in the psalm paraphrase goes back before Vatable's death which occurred in 1547 ; but there are reasonable grounds, as we have seen, for accepting this assumption. On the other hand, even if Buchanan did not know Vatable, there were ways and means of consulting the scholar's notes on the Hebrew text of the Psalms.

Secondly, we know that Buchanan possessed a copy of Sebastian Münste's *Dictionarium Hebraicum* (Basel, Froben, 1523) ; it was given him by Florentius Volusenus, at a date unknown, and the volume, now in Edinburgh University Library, bears the inscription : " Georgius Buchananus ex munificentia florentij voluseni ". J. M. Aitken, referring to this book, writes :

> As Florence Wilson died in 1546, it seems that this book must have been in Buchanan's possession in 1550, and the possibility that he obtained the book after leaving Portugal may be definitely excluded.[85]

But there is evidence of Volusenus being alive in Lyons in 1551, and he probably lived on some years longer. On the other hand, Volusenus, whom Buchanan knew in Paris back in the early 1530s, published two small volumes then, which are of interest in our context : *Psalmi quindecimi enarratio*, Paris, 1531, and *In psalmum nobis 50 Hebræis vero 51 . . . enarratio*, Paris, 1532. We do not know a great deal about the influence of Volusenus upon Buchanan, but it may have been considerable, and it would certainly seem that both men were interested in the Psalms early on in their Parisian career.[86] Incidentally, the Hebrew dictionary was not the only work by Sebastian Münster that Buchanan might have used ; his translation of the Psalms was also available.[87]

In the third place, whatever Buchanan's knowledge of Hebrew—and it may have been reasonable—there were various commentaries of a linguistic nature on which he could have drawn, and a number of which were in fact published by Robert Estienne ; Buchanan was closely connected with several members of the Estienne family. First of all, there is a dictionary of Hebrew phrases, of which the copy preserved in the University of St Andrews Library is traditionally believed to have belonged to Buchanan and contains some marginal notes and textual underlinings :

> *Phrases Hebraicæ, seu loquendi genera Hebraica quæ in Veteri testamento passim leguntur, ex commentariis Hebræorum, aliisque doctissimorum virorum scriptis explicata. Thesauri linguæ Hebraicæ altera pars.* Oliua Roberti Stephani, M.D.,LVIII.

Many of the phrases noted or underlined refer to the psalms, and one could see here possible sources for Buchanan's own versions. For instance, under

---

[85] J. M. Aitken, op. cit., p. 147.

[86] The existence of these two works, both extant in Cambridge University Library, has been revealed by Dr J. Baker-Smith ; it is to be hoped that his doctoral thesis on Florence Volusenus will be published in the not too distant future.

[87] *Liber Psalmorum cum translationibus quatuor et Paraphrasibus duobus. . . Interpretes sunt Autor editionis vulgatae D. Hieronymus, Felix Pratensis, Sebast. Monsterus. Paraphrastae Autor Chaldaeus, Ioannes Campensis . . .* Argentorati 1545 (Copy : O).

Benedicere, the first heading is *Benedicere* & *laudare*, *idem*, with *laudare* underlined and *laudare gratias agere* added in the margin. The first reference in the dictionary is to Psalm XXXIV, v. 1, *Benedicam Jehovæ* . . . which Buchanan renders *Laudabo Dominum*. Further research would be needed to afford substantial proof here ; moreover, there is bound to be some overlap between the various commentaries that were available to Buchanan ; and in any case, the Estienne phrase-book came out a long time after Buchanan had first taken an interest in the Psalms—some paraphrases had already gone into print.

There are two other volumes published by Estienne which may have proved useful to Buchanan, and particularly the first one, which appeared before the journey to Portugal. Both books give in parallel the *Vetus tralatio*, and the new, though the new is not always the same in each book. Detailed notes are given at the bottom of each page. The 1557 work is, however, more substantial ; it gives words in their Hebrew characters, and Vatable's collaboration is broadcast, whereas the 1546 compendium maintained a discreet anonymity :

> *Liber Psalmorum Davidis* : *annotationes in eosdem ex Hebræorum commentariis* . . . Lutetiæ, ex officina R. Stephani, 1546.

and *Liber Psalmorum Davidis. Tralatio duplux, Vetus* & *Nova. Hæc posterior, Sanctis Pagnini, partim ab ipso Pagnino recognita, partim ex Francisci Vatabli Hebraicarum litterarum professoris quondam Regii eruditissimis prælectionibus emendata* & *expolita. Adiecta sunt annotationes cum ex aliorum tralatione, tum vero ex commentariis Hebræorum ab ipso Vatablo diligenter excusis* : *quæ commentarii vice lectoribus esse poterunt.* Oliua Roberti Stephani. M.D.LVI (Colophon gives date anno M.D.LVII. Cal. Ian.)
(Both books can be consulted in O.)

A few random examples will, I think, show that Buchanan owes a great deal to the " new " translations and suggest the probability that he did in fact use these works of reference :[88] to begin with, LXI offers several possible echoes :

> LXI v. 2 VT   Exaudi Deus deprecationem meam
> NT57 *Audi* Deus *clamorem* meum (also NT 46)
> GB   *Audi vocantem* me bonus . . .

Audi is preferred to *exaudi*, and the nuance of *deprecationem* is dropped.

> v. 3 VT   A finibus terræ ad te *clamaui*
> NT57 Ab extremo terræ ad te *clamabo* (also NT 46)
> GB   Ad te *recurram* rebus in asperis.

Buchanan prefers the future tense of the NT.

> v. 6 VT   Quoniam tu Deus exaudisti orationem meam
> NT57 Quoniam tu Deus audisti *vota* mea
> GB   Qui lenis aurem das *precibus* meis
> Qui *vota* lætum ducis ad exitum.

---

[88] In the comparisons between the various texts, the following abbreviations are used : VT = Vetus tralatio ; NT = Nova tralatio, with 46 or 57 following to denote the year of publication ; GB = Buchanan's Paraphrase. Words relevant to the discussion are italicised.

Buchanan may well have followed the note on NT *vota*, defined as *preces* in grave circumstances.

LXX v. 3 VT   Confundantur & reuereantur qui quærunt animam
meam
NT57 Pudore afficiantur & *erubescant* quærentes animam
meam
GB   Qui meam quærunt animam, *erubescant.*

Buchanan has chosen the more picturesque, but also more accurate term. A striking example of his fidelity to the new translation will be found in LXXXI, vv. 3-5 :

VT   Sumite psalmum, & date tympanum : psalterium iu-
cundum cum cithara. Buccinate in Neomenia tuba,
in insigni die solennitas vestræ . . .
NT46 Sumite psalmum, date tympanum, citharam suauem
cum *nablo. Clangite* cornu, noua luna, *stato die.*
(in the notes : cornu, vel tuba . . . noua luna uel
calendis ipsis)
NT57 Sumite canticum, & date tympanum, citharam iu-
cundam cum *nebel. Clangite* in *calendis tuba*, in tem-
pore *constituto*, in die *festiuitatis* nostræ
(In the notes : quia *statutum* Israeli est, iudicium Deo
Iacob)
GB   Isacidum laudate Deum, pæana canentes
Ad tympani dulces modos.
Nec lyra, nec cessent genialia *nablia* : *festis*
Tuba calendis clangite.
Hunc læti celebrate diem, *stata* sacra ferentes.

The words underlined will show the similarities between Buchanan's para-phrase and the words used in the NT.

CV, which was revised in a number of details after it was first published, also affords some interesting illustrations of Buchanan's method of work :

v. 11 VT   Dicens, Tibi dabo Terram Chanaan, funiculum hære-
ditatis vestræ.
NT46 Dicens, Tibi tradam Chananæorum terram, ut sit tibi
hæreditaria *sors.*
GB   Quum tibi Chananæa (dixit)
Arua sorte diuidam.

Two points arise here : Buchanan has used *sors*, but he may also have re-membered a footnote on *terram* which suggests the use of the plural :

Heb. funem hæreditatis vestræ. Mutatio personæ,
pro sortem possessionis tuæ. Funis pro hæreditate,
Mutatur etiam singularis in pluralem quo facienda
esset distributio terræ pluribus.

And Buchanan has preferred to avoid *funis*. This psalm offers another good example, in that among other things a change of text is involved :

vv.31-2 VT   Dixit & venit *cynomyia*, & cinifes in omnibus finibus
eorum.
Posuit pluvias eorum grandinem : ignem comburen-
tem in terra ipsorum.

NT46 Eius etiam iussu venerunt omnis generis insecta &
pediculi per omnes fines eorum.
Et pro pluuiis eorum dedit grandinem, & ignem *flam-*
mantem in ipsorum terra.
(In the notes : Deus vertit *imbres* eorum in grandinem
& ignem urentem, uel, pro pluuia dedit grandinem
admisto fulmine)

GB   *Cyniphwn* cruenta passim obvolabant agmina
Instar *imbrium* ruebat *mista flamma* grandini
Arbores nudans comantes, flore, fronde, fructibus.

From the beginning the words *imbrium, mista, flamma* bear a marked resemblance to the vocabulary and notes of the NT ; but what is more interesting
is that Buchanan changed one of the lines in later editions to :

Et *pediculorum* ubique fœda erant examina

The hellenism *Cyniphwn*, so much nearer the VT, has been replaced by the
Latin term used in the NT.

One final example : in CX, v. 6, Buchanan writes :

Ducesque regnis imperantes *ditibus*
Sternet solo . . .

Though the commentary to NT57 has a footnote about " regionibus amplis-
simis ", it is only the 1546 volume that introduces the idea of wealth explicitly : " principes qui præsunt regionibus amplis. & *diuitibus*", and it
may well be that this is the source of Buchanan's epithet.

Clearly, a great deal more work has to be done on Buchanan's sources ;
but I believe that further research will confirm the impression that his
motives were by no means purely literary ; he was using contemporary
scholarship to make the understanding of the psalms more precise. He did
not always eschew the Vulgate and, obviously, considerations of a metrical
nature must on occasion have determined the choice of vocabulary ; but it
is not unreasonable to see in Buchanan's psalm paraphrases an attempt to
make the results of Biblical scholarship more widely known. Two factors
have perhaps tended to obscure this aspect of his work : on the one hand,
the pedagogic use of the paraphrases to instil better latinity into schoolchildren, and on the other, a reluctance to think that Buchanan's religious
views were very profound. Of course, there is nothing of the mystic in
Buchanan, and his personality often gives the impression of coldness, though
he had a remarkable gift for friendship. This does not mean that religion
meant nothing to him, and I am convinced that in fact one of the elements
that helped to bind Buchanan in friendship with many French scholars was
a persistent preoccupation with things religious. The paraphrases deserve
to be studied again in this light.

I. D. McFarlane

Oxford

III

THE THEME OF ILLUSION IN RONSARD'S *SONETS POUR HELENE* AND IN THE VARIANTS OF THE 1552 *AMOURS*

For many modern readers the *Sonets pour Helene* represent one of the major pinnacles of Ronsard's poetic achievement. Yet Ronsard himself gave the collection no particular prominence when he first published it in the 1578 edition of his *Œuvres*.[1] Nor would his public in the late sixteenth and early seventeenth centuries necessarily have shared our view ; we read, for instance, in the section devoted to Ronsard in the *Perroniana* that

> il ne faut pas s'estonner s'il n'a pas reüssy aux amours, aux sonnets, & aux petits vers, son esprit n'estoit porté qu'à representer des guerres, des sieges de ville, des combats ; . . . ses Sonnets ne sont pas bien excellents. . . Ce n'estoit pas son fait que des Sonnets, son esprit alloit plus haut ; ceux qui son[t] venus aprés luy s'y sont plus adonnez, & ont mieux reüssy aux choses d'amour que luy.[2]

Nowadays most people would probably exactly reverse this particular judgement, preferring his love-poetry to all the rest. Indeed, the *Sonets pour Helene*, remarkable for their piquant combination of elegantly stylised petrarchan themes and attitudes with sharp, often biting psychological realism, are perhaps more in tune with the ironical sensibility of the middle decades of the twentieth century than any other section of Ronsard's work. Ronsard's command of his medium, his ability to exploit for his own wry purposes the thematic and stylistic conventions within which he is writing, the nimbleness and confidence with which he sets up a richly suggestive counterpoint between the established metrical pattern of the sonnet on the one hand, and the rhythm of the meaning on the other,[3] undoubtedly reveal a poet at the height of his powers.

The *Sonets pour Helene* are not only a collection of poems about love : in a very important sense they are also about the pain, the impatient irritation of growing old—or at least, of growing irrevocably middle-aged. The military imagery in the *Sonets pour Helene*, for instance, which echoes

---

[1] This point is more fully discussed in Dr Malcolm Smith's recent edition of the 1587 *Sonnets pour Helene* in the Textes Littéraires Français series, Geneva and Paris, 1970, pp. 7-12.

[2] *Perroniana et Thuana*, Rouen, 1669², p. 270. Du Perron (1556-1618) delivered Ronsard's funeral oration. For Ronsard's reputation in the years following his death, see the first two chapters of R. A. Katz, *Ronsard's French Critics 1585-1828*, Geneva, 1966, which deal with the years 1585-1600 and 1601-1630 respectively. The passage quoted from the *Perroniana* is discussed on p. 50.

[3] What I have in mind here is, *mutatis mutandis*, the kind of phenomenon described by Robert Frost, writing of his own poetry : " there are the very regular pre-established accent and measure of blank verse ; and there are the very irregular accent and measure of speaking intonation. I am never more pleased than when I can get these into strained relation. I like to drag and break the intonation across the meter as waves first comb and then break stumbling on the shingle " (letter to John Cournos, 8 July 1914, in *Selected Letters of Robert Frost*, ed. L. Thompson, London, 1965, p. 128).

both the epic associations of the story of Helen of Troy and also, more closely, the use made of such imagery in Ovid's *Amores*, is repeatedly used by Ronsard in a thoroughly ironical fashion to emphasise the inappropriategess of the poet's situation—that of an old man trying to play a young man's game :

> Maintenant en Automne encore malheureux,
> Je vy comme au Printemps de nature amoureux, . . .
> Et ores que je deusse estre exempt du harnois,
> Mon Colonnel m'envoye à grands coups de carquois
> R'assieger Ilion pour conquerir Heleine.[4]

One of the most clearly stated themes in this portrait of the grey-haired lover, impatient at being enthralled again by love, and on occasion fiercely resentful of Helene's aloofness, is that of illusion—the acknowledgement, insistence even, that illusion and self-deception are inevitably present in the love-relationship. The *sententia* which ends sonnet XXIII in book II —" S'abuser en amour n'est pas mauvaise chose "—is perhaps the most striking expression of this theme. But it is not an isolated, uncharacteristic example ; on the contrary, it forms part of a clearly discernible sequence in which the emphasis given to the theme shifts significantly.

The theme of illusion first appears in the *Sonets pour Helene* at the end of the fifth sonnet in book I (" Helene sceut charmer avec son Nepenthe ").[5] In this sonnet the poet wishes that from their two loves some new plant might grow " Qui retienne noz noms pour eternelle foy, / Qu'obligé je me suis de servitude à toy ". But he corrects himself in the final tercet :

> O desir fantastiq, duquel je me deçoy,
> Mon souhait n'adviendra, puis qu'en vivant je voy
> Que mon amour me trompe, & qu'il n'a point de frere.

Here the poet is simply acknowledging, without further comment, that his wish is entirely fanciful and impossible of fulfilment, for in reality he knows that Helene does not return his love.

By sonnet XVIII of book I, however (" Je fuis les pas frayez du meschant populaire "),[6] there has been added to the straightforward acknowledgement by the poet that he deludes himself a marked note of willing

---

[4] Ronsard, *Œuvres complètes*, ed. P. Laumonier, Paris, 1914-1967, vol. XVII, p. 255 ; all references to Ronsard's works will be to this edition. See also the sonnet beginning " Comme un vieil combatant, qui ne veut plus s'armer " (ibid., p. 263), and the first quatrain of " Je m'enfuy du combat, ma bataille est desfaite " (ibid., p. 294). Cf. Ovid, *Amores*, I, ix, 1-4 :

> Militat omnis amans, et habet sua castra Cupido,
> Attice, crede mihi, militat omnis amans.
> quae bello est habilis, Veneri quoque convenit aetas.
> turpe senex miles, turpe senilis amor ;

and II, ix, 3-4, 19, 23-24, addressing Cupid :

> quid me, qui miles numquam tua signa reliqui,
> laedis, et in castris vulneror ipse meis ? . . .
> Fessus in acceptos miles deducitur agros ; . . .
> me quoque, qui totiens merui sub amore puellae,
> defunctum placide vivere tempus erat.

[5] *Œuvres complètes*, vol. XVII, pp. 198-199.

[6] Ibid., p. 211.

acquiescence in the self-deception. Using motifs enriched by Petrarchan and Horatian echoes,[7] the poet presents himself as leading a solitary life in his misery, accompanied only by " Amour mon secretaire ". Sometimes, to comfort himself, he imagines that Helene might be thinking of him, or even softening in her attitude towards him. He knows that such a thing cannot really be so ; but, he ends,

> Encor que je me trompe, abusé du contraire,
> Pour me faire plaisir, Helene, je le croy.

The comfort afforded by the dream, even though the poet knows it to be an illusion, is yet a source of clear pleasure to him.

But on the next occasion when the theme of illusion appears, towards the end of the first book (sonnet LIV, " J'attachay des bouquets de cent mille couleurs "),[8] it is treated rather more ambiguously. Here, echoing an epigram from the *Greek Anthology*,[9] the poet hopes that the petals of the flowers which he has hung over Helene's door and which were " arrosez " with his tears, will fall upon her as she leaves her room next day, ". . . de telle sorte / Que son chef soit mouillé de l'humeur de mes pleurs ". The tercets, however, develop a very different idea from this graceful gesture of the languishing lover :

> Je reviendray demain. Mais si la nuict, qui ronge
> Mon cœur, me la donnoit par songe entre mes bras,
> Embrassant pour le vray l'idole du mensonge,
> Soulé d'un faux plaisir je ne reviendrois pas.

The illusion and self-deception involved in the dream-experience are heavily stressed in this passage, and the irony of the poet's situation is fully brought out by the deliberate ambiguity of the two lines which close the poem :

[7] See Petrarch, sonnet XXXV, lines 1-2 (*Opere*, ed. E. Bigi, Milan, 1964², p. 32) :
Solo e pensoso i piú deserti campi
vo mesurando a passi tardi e lenti
—yet " Amor " never leaves him ; and Horace, *Carmina*, III, i, 1-4 :
Odi profanum vulgus et arceo ;
favete linguis : carmina non prius
audita Musarum sacerdos
virginibus puerisque canto.

[8] *Œuvres complètes*, vol. XVII, p. 244.

[9] ΕΠΙΓΡΑΜΜΑΤΑ ΕΡΩΤΙΚΑ, no. 145 :
Αὐτοῦ μοι, στέφανοι, παρὰ δικλίσι ταῖσδε κρεμαστοὶ
μίμνετε, μὴ προπετῶς φύλλα τινασσόμενοι,
οὓς δακρύοις κατέβρεξα· κάτομβρα γὰρ ὄμματ' ἐρώντων.
Ἀλλ' ὅταν οἰγομένης αὐτὸν ἴδητε θύρης,
στάξαθ' ὑπὲρ κεφαλῆς ἐμὸν ὑετόν, ὡς ἂν ἄμεινον
ἡ ξανθή γε κόμη τἄμα πίῃ δάκρυα.

(Là, mes couronnes, suspendues à ces battants, restez là sans vous hâter de secouer vos pétales que mes larmes ont mouillés, car il y a des pluies dans les yeux des amoureux. Mais dès que, la porte ouverte, vous l'aurez aperçu, distillez sur sa tête la rosée de mes larmes, pour que mieux s'en abreuve sa blonde chevelure.) *Anthologie grecque* (*première partie : Anthologie palatine*, livre V), ed. P. Waltz and J. Guillon, Paris, 1928, pp. 70-71. The editors add in a footnote : " Il faut admettre ou qu'il s'agit d'une jeune fille parlant de son amant ou que nous avons là une épigramme pédérastique ; la seconde explication nous paraît plus vraisemblable ". For a discussion of Ronsard's use of the *Greek Anthology* in the *Sonets pour Helene*, see J. Hutton, *The Greek Anthology in France and in the Latin writers of the Netherlands up to the year 1800*, Ithaca, 1946, pp. 363-374.

Voyez combien ma vie est pleine de trespas,
Quand tout mon reconfort ne depend que du songe.

Line 13 forms in part a half-playful allusion to the familiar petrarchist paradox in which, hyperbolically, the lover's indissoluble attachment to his *dolce nemica* is presented as the source both of his life and of his death. It is also perhaps an attempt to convey (again, in well-established imagery) the near-ecstatic culmination of the dreamed embrace.[10] Thus, on one level the poet's life is full of pain and wretchedness, since his only solace is the illusory one provided by dreams. Yet on another level it is full of delight, since the satisfaction of his feelings towards Helene depends not on reality, but on complaisant illusion. The final rhyme, however, inevitably recalls the harsher, more unequivocal, " idole du mensonge " of line 11, reinforcing, even in the moment of asserting the value of the dream, its inescapably deceptive nature.

In this last sonnet the poet's self-deception had been presented in the particular form of a *songe amoureux*, a dream in which he could make love to his normally aloof and distant mistress. This motif Ronsard exploits again in his fullest treatment in the *Sonets pour Helene* of the theme of illusion, namely sonnet XXIII of the second book, to which I have already referred briefly :[11]

Ces longues nuicts d'hyver, où la Lune ocieuse
Tourne si lentement son char tout à l'entour,
Où le Coq si tardif nous annonce le jour,
Où la nuict semble un an à l'ame soucieuse :
Je fusse mort d'ennuy sans ta forme douteuse,
Qui vient par une feinte alleger mon amour,
Et faisant, toute nue, entre mes bras sejour,
Me pipe doucement d'une joye menteuse.
Vraye tu es farouche, & fiere en cruauté :
De toy fausse on jouyst en toute privauté.
Pres ton mort je m'endors, pres de luy je repose :
Rien ne m'est refusé. Le bon sommeil ainsi
Abuse par le faux mon amoureux souci.
S'abuser en amour n'est pas mauvaise chose.[12]

The *songe amoureux* is a subject which had been made familiar by the *Greek Anthology*,[13] by petrarchist and neo-Latin poets, as well as by Ronsard himself (in earlier poems) and other sixteenth-century French poets.[14] What

---

[10] For another instance of this last usage, see the final tercet of Ronsard's sonnet " Quand en songeant ma follastre j'acolle " (*Œuvres complètes*, vol. IV, p. 100) :
Combien de fois doulcement irrité,
Suis-je ore mort, ore resuscité,
Parmy l'odeur de mile & mile roses ?

[11] See above, p. 64.

[12] *Œuvres complètes*, vol. XVII, pp. 264-265.

[13] See ΕΠΙΓΡΑΜΜΑΤΑ ΕΡΩΤΙΚΑ, nos. 2 and 243.

[14] See the valuable discussion in H. Weber, *La Création poétique au XVIe siècle en France*, Paris, 1956, vol. I, pp. 356-366, where the author analyses and compares poems by Sannazaro, Bembo, Magny, Baïf, Du Bellay, Ronsard, and Grévin. References to the appearance of the theme in neo-Latin poetry can be found in Ronsard, *Œuvres complètes*, vol. IV, p. 33, n. 4.

is perhaps most noticeable about Ronsard's treatment of the subject in this sonnet is the extent to which the account of the sensuous delight afforded by the dream (line 7) is hedged about by elements which underline very firmly the negative aspects of the experience. First, the opening quatrain describes with great vividness the oppressiveness and seeming interminability of winter nights to the insomniac lover : the moon in her movement across the sky is wearisomely sluggish ; even the cock is slow to crow. Not only is the winter setting here the very antithesis of the expected norm in love-poetry—since spring is traditionally the season associated with love— but also the lover's complaint at the almost unbearable length of the nights is the reverse of the wish often expressed by poets evoking a night spent (whether in reality or in imagination) with their mistress : namely, that it might last for ever.[15]

In addition, even when describing Helene lying with him in his dream " toute nue, entre [ses] bras ", the poet recognises right from the beginning that it is all merely an illusion : "... ta forme douteuse, / Qui vient par une feinte alleger mon amour, / ... / Me pipe doucement d'une joye menteuse ". The positive notations (*alleger, doucement, joye*) are each sharply offset by negative ones : *par une feinte, Me pipe, menteuse*. The pleasure and peace brought by making love to Helene are greatly diminished by the poet's continual awareness that they are illusory feelings :

Vraye tu es farouche, & fiere en cruauté :
De toy fausse on jouyst en toute privauté.

The rhythm ensures that the word " fausse " here has considerable emphasis and prominence.

The full irony of the poet's experience is made apparent in the final tercet. The extent of his delight is summed up in an understated, matter-of-fact hemistich : " Rien ne m'est refusé ". The rest of the tercet offers contrasting reflections on this situation. On the one hand kind, benevolent sleep — whose kindness was precisely to bring the poet's mistress to his bed — is but a deceiver in fact. Yet from another point of view there are compensations even in this : since reality offers the poet no satisfaction, his dream deceptive illusion though it is, is better than nothing.

---

[15] Cf., for instance, the end of Ronsard's sonnet " Je vouldroy bien richement jaunissant " (*Œuvres complètes*, vol. IV, pp. 23-24) : " Et vouldroy bien que ceste nuict encore / Durast tousjours ...". Also Petrarch, sestina XXII, " A qualunque animale alberga in terra ", lines 31-33 (*Opere*, p. 16) :
Con lei foss'io da che si parte il sole,
e non ci vedess'altri che le stelle,
sol una notte, e mai non fosse l'alba ;
Giraud de Borneil, " Rei glorios, verais lums e clardatz ", lines 31-32 (in M. Raynouard, *Choix des poésies originales des troubadours*, Paris, 1818, vol. III, p. 314) :
Bel dos companh, tan soy en ric sojorn
Qu'ieu no volgra mais fos alba ni jorn ;
Ovid, *Amores*, I, xiii, 3, 9, 27-28 :
Quo properas, Aurora ? mane ! ...
quo properas, ingrata viris, ingrata puellis ? ...
optavi quotiens, ne nox tibi cedere vellet,
ne fugerent vultus sidera mota tuos !

In the final occurrence of the theme of illusion in the *Sonets pour Helene*, however, the experience of the dream and the consciousness of its falsity are taken very clearly as an image of the whole love-relationship, but with little suggestion now that there is any comfort to be gained from the illusion which the dream offers. In a pair of sonnets at the end of the second book, the poet informs Helene in a very " anti-petrarchan " fashion[16] that he is withdrawing from the *amoureux combat* : he is weary of obtaining no " recompense " from her, and anyway, he says, he is too old to go on any longer. In one of these poems (" Adieu, cruelle, adieu, je te suis ennuyeux "),[17] the dream-motif again provides the theme of the final bitter reflection on the poet's mingled foolishness and misery. He has had enough of it all, he is giving up : " Te serve qui voudra, je m'en vay . . .". Furthermore, reason is recalling him, and he determines to nurture no longer the child Cupid, whose victims are merely so many " credules ", rising to the bait of " Une plaisante farce, une belle mensonge, / Un plaisir pour cent maux, qui s'envole soudain "—which are all that love is, in fact. In contrast to this,

> . . . il se faut resoudre & tenir pour certain
> Que l'homme est malheureux, qui se repaist d'un songe.

The maxim rings out bleakly (with the bleakness again reinforced by the *songe-mensonge* rhyme), offering no comfort, even in illusion. We are now at the opposite extreme from the " Pour me faire plaisir, Helene, je le croy " of book I ; indeed, the almost belligerent bitterness implicit in the present passage provides one of the dominant notes at the end of this collection, contrasting sharply with the guarded expansiveness of the opening.[18]

[16] The expression of " anti-petrarchan " attitudes within a basically petrarchan framework is a marked feature of the *Sonets pour Helene*. The theme is announced in the first sonnet of the collection (*Œuvres complètes*, vol. XVII, pp. 194-195) : contrast lines 9-10,

> Vous seule me plaisez : j'ay par election
> Et non à la volee aimé vostre jeunesse,

with lines 13-14 of Petrarch's sonnet CCXLVII (" Parrà forse ad alcun che 'n lodar quella ", *Opere*, p. 179) :

> . . . Amor la spinge e tira,
> non per elezion ma per destino.

(" La " is the poet's " lingua mortale ", stimulated by love to sing the praises of the divine Laura.)

This aspect of the *Sonets pour Helene* is stressed by Mary Morrison in her article " Ronsard and Desportes ", in *Bibliotheque d'Humanisme et Renaissance* XXVIII (1966), pp. 303 ff.

[17] *Œuvres complètes*, vol. XVII, p. 293.

[18] Similar treatments of the theme of illusion are to be found in some of the sonnets which in 1578 appeared under the title of *Amours diverses*, but were inserted in the *Sonets pour Helene* in 1584. Cf. *Amours diverses*, sonnet L, lines 7-8 (*Œuvres complètes*, vol. XVII, p. 329) :

> . . . Malheureux est qui aime,
> Malheureux qui se laisse à l'Amour decevoir !

and sonnet LIV, lines 1-4 (ibid., p. 333) :

> Amour, je pren congé de ta menteuse escole
> Où j'ay perdu l'esprit, la raison & le sens,
> Où je me suis trompé, où j'ay gasté mes ans,
> Où j'ay mal employé ma jeunesse trop folle.

Sonnet XXXVIII (ibid., pp. 317-318) is also based in part on related themes ; this poem, however, was not subsequently incorporated in the *Sonets pour Helene* :

Yet all the poems from the *Sonets pour Helene* which I have discussed offer a marked contrast in emphasis with sonnets dealing with comparable themes in the *Amours* of 1552. There, it is the joy and delight brought by the dreamed illusion which are more usually insisted upon, rather than its deceptive, illusory qualities. In sonnet CI, for instance (" Quand en songeant ma follastre j'acolle "),[19] the dream-experience is accepted totally, without question ; throughout the poem—which is filled with an atmosphere of richly languorous physicality—the only kind of reality to be presented is that of the poet's dream. It is as though the particular quality of his erotic sensations can be conveyed to the reader only through a presentation of his dreaming state, in that they are enhanced, not invalidated, by being dreamed:

> Mon dieu, quel heur, & quel contentement,
> M'a fait sentir ce faux recollement,
> Changeant ma vie en cent metamorphoses :
> Combien de fois doulcement irrité,
> Suis-je ore mort, ore resuscité,
> Parmy l'odeur de mile & mile roses ?[20]

Similarly, sonnet CLIX (" Il faisoit chault, & le somme coulant "),[21] which conveys so beautifully, in Henri Weber's words, ' la chaleur d'une après-midi d'été qui invite au sommeil et favorise le rêve voluptueux ",[22] concentrates on the sensuous delights which the poet enjoys. His mistress in his dream,

> Panchant soubz moy son bel ivoyre blanc,
> Et mitirant sa langue fretillarde,
> Me baisotoyt d'une lévre mignarde,
> Bouche sur bouche & le flanc sus le flanc.

In both these poems the dream itself is presented to the reader with great vividness ; there is no moment of cruel awakening into cold reality— indeed, both sonnets end on a crescendo of sensuous evocation—and the possible illusoriness of the experience is hardly alluded to at all. But even in those poems where the illusory quality of the dream does play a more important part, it is not allowed to dominate the poem (as we have seen it do in the *Sonets pour Helene*), nor even substantially to diminish the pleasure which the dream brings. In sonnet XXIX, for instance (" Si mille oeilletz,

Chacun me dit, Ronsard, ta maistresse n'est telle
Comme tu la descris. Certes je n'en sçay rien :
Je suis devenu fol, mon esprit n'est plus mien,
Je ne puis discerner la laide de la belle . . .
    Je ne sçaurois juger, tant la fureur me suit :
    Je suis aveugle & fol : un jour m'est une nuict,
    Et la fleur d'un Chardon m'est une belle Rose.
For a detailed discussion of the effects of the 1584 additions on the structure of the *Sonets pour Helene*, see D. Stone, *Ronsard's Sonnet Cycles : A Study in Tone and Vision*, New Haven and London, 1966, pp. 227-243.
    [19] *Œuvres complètes*, vol. IV, p. 100.
    [20] For a more detailed analysis of " Quand en songeant ma follastre j'acolle ", see my contribution to *The Art of Criticism : essays in French Literary Analysis*, ed. P. H. Nurse, Edinburgh, 1969, pp. 18-26.
    [21] *Œuvres complètes*, vol. IV, pp. 151-152.
    [22] *La Création poétique* . . ., vol. I, p. 363.

si mille liz j'embrasse ")‚[23] the quatrains are devoted entirely to an account of the joy which the poet owes to his " Songe divin ". This is presented first through the strongly sensuous image of the poet embracing myriads of flowers—an image which not only alludes to (and transcends) the familiar petrarchist likening of the loved woman's complexion to beautiful flowers, but also serves to prepare for the equally powerful image, already well-established in erotic poetry, of the vine eagerly embracing the branch on which it climbs.[24] The poet's delight is then described in more generalised terms :

> Si le souci ne jaunist plus ma face,
> Si le plaisir fonde en moy son sejour,
> Si j'ayme mieulx les ombres que le jour,
> Songe divin, cela vient de ta grace

and only in the tercets is it lessened, as he indicates his disappointment at the inevitable disappearance of his dream. Yet even here, the air of almost languorous ease in which the final images appear allows one to feel that the mood of joy and sensuous exhilaration still lingers very powerfully in the poet's being :

> Et tu me fuis au meillieu de mon bien,
> Comme l'esclair qui se finist en rien,
> Ou comme au vent s'esvanouit la nuë.

There is no trace of harshness or bitterness here ; it is the vivid memory of delight which predominates.

Similarly, in the next sonnet (XXX, " Ange divin, qui mes playes embasme ")‚[25] the poet acknowledges that his dream is an illusion, but again he concentrates rather on what is positive, on the delights he enjoys in the dream. In the opening quatrain the poet wonders which gate of heaven his dream has passed through to reach him—through the gate of ivory, through which only deceitful visions pass, or through the gate of horn, from which true prophecies emerge.[26] The image of his " Dame " disappears, and in the tercets he appeals to the " idole " to stay :

> . . . Atten encor un peu,
> Que vainement je me soye repeu
> De ce beau sein, dont l'appetit me ronge,

---

[23] Œuvres complètes, vol. IV, pp. 32-33.

[24] Cf. the second of Jean Second's Basia, which begins :
> Vicina quantum vitis lascivit in ulmo,
> Et tortiles per ilicem
> Brachia proceram stringunt immensa corymbi,
> Tantum, Neaera, si queas
> In mea nexilibus proserpere colla lacertis,
> Tali, Neaera, si queam
> Candida perpetuum nexu tua colla ligare,
> Jungens perenne basium . . .

(J. Second, Les Baisers et l'Epithalame, ed. M. Rat, Paris, 1938, p. 4. The notes [pp. 210-211] quote passages in which this image occurs from Horace, Ovid, Ronsard, Belleau, Tasso, Du Bellay, and others.)

[25] Œuvres complètes, vol. IV, pp. 33-34.

[26] See Homer, Odyssey, XIX, 559-567, and Virgil, Aeneid, VI, 893-896.

Et de ces flancz, qui me font trespasser :
Sinon d'effect, seuffre au moins que par songe
Toute une nuict je les puisse embrasser.

Again, the poem ends on a strongly positive note (despite the word " vaine-ment "), with the evocation in vivid physical detail of the dreamed embrace.

Indeed, it is only when we examine the amendments which Ronsard made to some of the sonnets in the 1552 *Amours* for the editions of his collected *Œuvres* published in 1578 and in 1584 that the emphasis on illusion so characteristic of the *Sonets pour Helene* can be seen to reappear. It seems significant, yet hardly surprising, perhaps, that there should be some parallel-ism between the themes of the new poems and those of the amendments to old poems. Sometimes the changes in wording are relatively slight ; but the change in meaning is always quite marked.

In sonnet XLI, for instance (" Ores l'effroy & ores l'esperance "),[27] the antithetical balance of the lover's opposite-and-equal emotions is summed up towards the end of the second quatrain in a line describing him as " Heur-eusement de moy mesme trompeur ". In 1578 the antithesis suggested by *heureusement/trompeur* is eliminated, and the implications of " trompeur " become more fully underlined : " Pour estre en vain de moy-mesme trom-peur ". The change in emphasis is very clear.

Sonnet LXV,[28] on the other hand, presents the poet's relationship with his mistress in terms of the Circe-Ulysses situation : his reason is blinded by love. In 1552 the first two lines of the sonnet read :

Du tout changé ma Circe enchanteresse
Dedens ses fers m'enferre emprisonné.

In 1578 the opening phrase was changed to " Trompé d'esprit, ma Circe . . .", and in 1584 to " Pipé d'Amour, ma Circe . . .". Again, sonnet LXXXV (" D'Amour ministre, & de perseverance "),[29] which, with a nega-tivity of attitude unusual for Ronsard in 1552, is a harsh and bitter attack on " Malencontreuse & meschante esperance ", ends with an allusion to the story of Pandora and her box. Once Pandora had opened the box and re-leased all the evils it contained upon mankind, only Hope remained at the bottom of it :

Il [Jupiter] te laissa, Harpye, & salle oyseau,
Cropir au fond du Pandorin vaisseau,
Pour enfieller le plus doulx miel des hommes.

In 1584 the last two lines were altered to :

Seule par force au profond du vaisseau
Que Pandore eut pour decevoir les hommes.

All mention of " le plus doulx miel des hommes " has now disappeared, and instead the theme of deceit and deception—already implicit in the Pandora myth—is given prominence as the last impression which the poem leaves with its readers.

[27] *Œuvres complètes*, vol. IV, p. 44.
[28] Ibid., pp. 66-67.
[29] Ibid., pp. 85-86.

Another very clear instance of what seems to be a consistent pattern in Ronsard's revisions is provided by sonnet CXXV.[30] This poem takes the form of a lament by Narcissus (an extreme case, of course, of the illusion-in-love situation) at his own predicament : *must* I waste away, he asks, obsessed by the image of my own face ? In 1552 the sonnet began :

> Que laschement vous me trompez, mes yeulx,
> Enamourez d'une figure vaine.

In 1578 the first line was altered to : " En vous trompant, vous me trompez, mes yeux ", and in 1584 to : " En m'abusant je me trompe les yeux ". Fernand Desonay, commenting on the variants of this sonnet in his *Ronsard poète de l'amour*, regrets the disappearance of " l'attaque véhémente de la leçon originale . . . [qui] fait place, en 1578, puis en 1584, à de lourdes tournures gérondives ".[31] One can see also that what Ronsard is doing here is progressively reinforcing the theme of illusion to the point at which the illusion becomes clear self-deception. Initially Narcissus had blamed his eyes for deceiving him in such a despicable fashion (presumably there is an oblique reference in this to the petrarchist lover's traditional vulnerability to sense-impressions of sight). In 1578 his eyes are no longer blamed ; Narcissus acknowledges that they are themselves deceived, but points out that in allowing themselves to be deceived, they deceive him, too. Finally, in 1584, the responsibility for the deception is completely internalised : the deception is quite explicitly *self*-deception now, and the eyes are deceived by the self, rather than deceivers of it.[32]

Not surprisingly, the two sonnets which I quoted earlier as cases where the illusory nature of the poet's dream, though acknowledged, is not allowed to diminish or invalidate the delights it brings him,[33] are also revised in 1578 in such a way that the theme of illusion is reinforced. In sonnet XXIX (" Si mille œilletz, si mille liz j'embrasse ") the passage in the first tercet indicating the coming interruption of the poet's dream had originally read :

> Mais ce portraict qui nage dans mes yeulx,
> Fraude tousjours ma joye entrerompuë.

In 1578 the phrase " qui nage dans mes yeulx ", with its attractively voluptuous associations, is replaced by " qui me trompe les yeux ". It is a small change in wording ; but the change in tone is very marked.

A similar change of tone is brought about by the amendments to the next sonnet (XXX, " Ange divin, qui mes playes embasme "). In the poet's appeal to the dream to remain, he had originally acknowledged its illusori-

---

[30] Ibid., p. 122.

[31] F. Desonay, *Ronsard poète de l'amour*, Brussels, 1952-1959, vol. I, p. 247. Desonay's overall attitude towards Ronsard's revisions of the early *Amours* is that " le Ronsard qui se corrige apparaît souvent sous les traits de l'éteigneur des ferveurs lyriques " (ibid., p. 245).

[32] In the first posthumous edition (1587) this development towards the self's acceptance of responsibility for the deception is to some slight extent reversed, for the blame is now ascribed to hope : " Trompé d'espoir, je me trompe les yeux ".

[33] See above, p. 70.

ness, but only to pass on to emphasise the intensity of his physical desire
and delight :

> Las, où fuis tu ? Atten encor un peu,
> Que vainement je me soye repeu
> De ce beau sein, dont l'appetit me ronge, . . .

Relatively minor modifications were made in 1567 (" sein " became " corps ",
for instance), but in 1578 the changes are more striking :

> Demeure Songe, arreste encor un peu.
> Trompeur, atten que je me sois repeu
> Du vain portrait dont l'appetit me ronge.

The sensuous elements of the dream are now played down (the " beau sein "
and " beau corps " of the earlier versions are replaced by the much less
specific " vain portrait "),[34] and at the same time it is emphasised more
firmly than before that the dream is merely an illusion. The idea contained
originally in the single adverb " vainement " is now spread over two lines,
and the first of the two words which replace it (" Trompeur ") is given
considerable stress by its position at the beginning of the line, so that it
seems to overshadow quite markedly the delight which the poet had conveyed through his account of the dream.

Yet perhaps the most significant and extensive revisions of this kind are
those which Ronsard made to a sonnet which is particularly conspicuous,
in that it opens the collection and thus sets the tone for what follows. The
1552 version reads :

> Qui voudra voyr comme un Dieu me surmonte,
> Comme il m'assault, comme il se fait vainqueur,
> Comme il r'enflamme, & r'englace mon cuœur,
> Comme il reçoit un honneur de ma honte,
> Qui voudra voir une jeunesse prompte
> A suyvre en vain l'object de son malheur,
> Me vienne voir : il voirra ma douleur,
> Et la rigueur de l'Archer qui me donte.
> Il cognoistra combien la raison peult
> Contre son arc, quand une foys il veult
> Que nostre cuœur son esclave demeure :
> Et si voirra que je suis trop heureux,
> D'avoir au flanc l'aiguillon amoureux,
> Plein du venin dont il fault que je meure.[35]

Appropriately enough, the sonnet begins with an allusion to a petrarchan
formula,[36] and ends, as is characteristic with Ronsard in the 1552 Amours,

[34] Henri and Catherine Weber, among others, have pointed out that in the course
of his revisions " Souvent Ronsard atténue la précision sensuelle et le caractère charnel
du désir. . . Cependant les corrections de ce genre ne sont pas systématiques " (Ronsard, Les Amours, ed. H. amd C. Weber, Paris, 1963, p. L). The present poem illustrates
their last point, also, for in line 12 (" Et de ces flancz qui me font trespasser ") " ces
flancz " become " ces yeux " in 1567, but " ce corps " in 1578.

[35] Œuvres complètes, vol. IV, pp. 5-6.

[36] Sonnet CCXLVIII, lines 1-2 (Opere, p. 180) :

> Chi vuol veder quantunque pò Natura
> e 'l Ciel tra noi, venga a mirar costei . . .

Petrarch is focusing the reader's attention on the wondrous beauty of Laura ; whereas

with an emphasis on the positive aspects of the experience which the lover is about to recount ; he delights, in fact, in the pain which love causes him. But in 1584 the tercets are completely reworked :[37]

> Il cognoistra qu'Amour est sans raison,
> Un doux abus, une belle prison,
> Un vain espoir que de vent nous vient paistre,
> Et cognoistra que l'homme se deçoit
> Quand plein d'erreur un aveugle il reçoit
> Pour sa conduite, un enfant pour son maistre.

Desonay points out that, originally, " toutes les rimes des tercets faisaient sonner le son ' eu ' (' peult-veult-demeure-heureux-amoureux-meure '), rappelant la rime masculine en ' -eur ' des quatrains " ; whereas from 1567 onwards, " [les] corrections successives . . . introduisent un nouveau jeu de rimes dans les tercets, mais ralentissent plutôt le mouvement ".[38] Equally striking on another level is the change of emphasis in the meaning of the poem, and thus, it would seem, in the attitude with which Ronsard wishes the reader to approach the whole collection. At the end of the *Sonets pour Helene* the poet had expressed his intention to cut himself off from " cest Enfant qui me ronge, / Qui les credules prend comme un poisson à l'hain ".[39] In the 1584 revision of the present poem, the illusion and self-deception involved in the state of enslavement to Cupid are similarly stressed. Love is an " abus " (though with its *douceurs*, certainly) ; it is a vain, illusory hope, offering us nothing more substantial than the empty air ; it is a form

Ronsard invites his readers to contemplate the effects of love upon the poet. Parallels for Ronsard's particular use of this formula can be found in the sonnet by Lodovico Dolce (1508-?1566), " Chi uuol ueder raccolto in un soggetto ", lines 9-11 (this poem appeared in the first volume of the Giolito anthology of *Rime diverse di molti eccellentiss. avttori nvovamente raccolte*, Venice, 1545, p. 310 ; Ronsard's copy of the second edition (1546) of this volume, containing his own marginal annotations, is in the Bibliothèque Nationale) :

> Sapra, si come Amor l'anima fura,
> Come l'ancide & le risana, & come
> Dolce è morir & uiuer in tal nodo ;

and in Pontus de Tyard, *Erreurs Amoureuses* (1549), sonnet II :

> Qui veut sçavoir en quante, et quelle sorte
> Amour cruel travaille les esprits
> De ceux, qui sont de son ardeur espris,
> Et, le servant, quel fruit on en rapporte :
> Qu'il vienne voir ma peine ardente et forte,
> En discourant ces miens piteux escris :
> Car mes helas, et mes souspirans cris
> Descouvriront la douleur que je porte.
> Il me verra craindre, et puis esperer,
> En desir croistre, et soudain empirer,
> Changer cent fois le jour de passion.
> Il me verra alors, qu'Amour se joue
> De mon mal'heur, sur l'amoureuse roue,
> Souffrir le mal d'un dolent Ixion.

(*Œuvres poétiques complètes*, ed. J. C. Lapp, Paris, 1966, p. 10.)

[37] The amendments made for the 1567 and 1578 editions of the *Œuvres* do not affect substantially the overall meaning of the tercets ; see *Œuvres complètes*, loc. cit., for details.

[38] *Ronsard poète de l'amour*, vol. I, p. 249.

[39] See above, p. 68.

of self-deception, and the lover is a man " plein d'erreur ". This markedly negative tone seems to me hardly to have been present in the poem at all in 1552. Then, the sonnet had ended with an elegantly phrased evocation of the familiar wounded stag image,[40] expressing a kind of gratified acceptance of the pain of love. The potential harshness of the reference to the poisoned arrow in the last line is largely muted by the easy, relaxed rhythm of the end of the sonnet, as it fades away into the final languishing " je meure ". In 1584, however, the sonnet seems to rise in the last tercet to a peak of near-bitterness and resentment which is not unlike the mood of the end of the *Sonets pour Helene*. The poet's anguish is conveyed now not only by the actual meaning of the words, but also by the awkward, yet strangely moving *enjambement* from line 13 to 14, and the resultant ending, out-of-step almost, on the ironical " un enfant pour son maistre ".

Strong emphasis on the inescapability of illusion and self-deception in the experience of love appears only rarely in Ronsard's poetry before the *Sonets pour Helene*. Indeed, the use of something close to this theme at the end of the elegy advising Amadis Jamyn to resist, like Ulysses, " le chant de la Serene ", which Ronsard inserted among the last few poems of the second book of *Amours* in 1567, is strikingly unusual :

> " L'Amour n'est rien qu'ardente frenaisie,
> " Qui de fumée emplist la fantaisie
> " D'erreur, de vent & d'un songe importun,
> " Car le songer & l'Amour ce n'est qu'un.[41]

The sentiments expressed and implied in the last line would not seem out of place in the *Sonets pour Helene*, eleven years later. There the theme of illusion forms part of a whole network of negatively coloured motifs which measure the distance between the young man's bounding enthusiasm for the experience of love, as expressed in the 1552 *Amours*, and the rueful, wounded withdrawal from that experience recounted in the *Sonets pour Helene*. As I have tried to show, the same negative colouring can be traced in the revisions which Ronsard made late in his writing life to his first collection of love-sonnets. The rewriting is not so extensive, nor always so radical, that it is in danger of reversing the predominatingly positive aspects of that work. Its effect is rather to bring about very clear modifications of emphasis at certain points, which serve, with the *Sonets pour Helene*, to underline the extent to which Ronsard's confidence in the full validity of the aesthetic and emotional experience of love has changed since the early 1550's.

GRAHAME CASTOR

Cambridge

[40] Cf., for instance, the emblem which precedes *dizain* 159 of Scève's *Délie*.

[41] *Œuvres complètes*, vol. XIV, pp. 81-83. Cf. also, from the 1560 *Premier Livre des Poemes*, " Le Cyclope amoureux ", where the Cyclops tells himself that instead of bewailing his unrequited love for Galatea, it would be better to concentrate on looking after his sheep, or to love someone else, or even to
> feindre dans toimesmes
> Que tu es bien aymé de celle que tu aymes :
> Car feindre d'estre aymé (puis que mieux on ne peut)
> Allege bien souvent l'amoureux qui se veult
> Soymesmes se tromper, se garissant la playe
> Aussi bien par le faux que par la chose vraye.

(*Œuvres complètes*, vol. X, p. 290.)

IV

SOME SOURCES AND TECHNIQUES
OF SOURCE ADAPTATION IN THE POETRY OF
JEAN-ANTOINE DE BAÏF

Whilst Mathieu Augé-Chiquet's comprehensive work on Jean-Antoine de Baïf[1] gave consideration to the sources of a wide range of the poet's extensive and diverse output, nevertheless the vast majority of both past and more recent research has tended to concentrate on the models of Baïf's *Amours*.[2] It is true that some scholars have directed their attention, either in the course of specific studies on Baïf or in more general studies of a genre, to the sources of his eclogues,[3] his mythological narrative poems based on Ovid[4] and his cosmological poem *Le Premier des Meteores*.[5] Again other research has examined the influence exerted on Baïf by Catullus,[6] Ronsard[7] and *The Greek Anthology*,[8] but there still remain areas of his poetry where work is needed to establish sources and to assess the extent and nature of spheres of influence.[9]

[1] Mathieu Augé-Chiquet, *La Vie, les Idées et l'Œuvre de Jean-Antoine de Baïf*, Paris, Hachette ; Toulouse, Privat, 1909. (Reprinted Slatkine Reprints, Geneva, 1969).

[2] Francesco Torraca, *Gl' imitatori stranieri di Jacopo Sannazaro*, Rome, Loescher, 1882 ; Francesco Flamini, " Di alcune inosservate imitazioni italiane in poeti francesi del Cinquecento ", in *Atti del Congresso internazionale di scienze storiche*, Rome, Accademia dei Lincei, 1904, Vol. IV, p. 161 ; E. S. Ingraham, *The sources of les Amours de Jean-Antoine de Baïf*, Columbus, Ohio, Fred J. Heer, 1905 ; Joseph Vianey, *Le Pétrarquisme en France au XVIe siècle*, Montpellier, Coulet, 1909 (reprinted Slatkine Reprints, Geneva, 1969) ; *Les Amours de Jean-Antoine de Baïf (Amours de Méline)*, édition critique publiée par Mathieu Augé-Chiquet, Paris, Hachette ; Toulouse, Privat, 1909 ; M. Augé-Chiquet, *Jean-Antoine de Baïf et Marc-Antonio Flaminio*, Clermont-Ferrand, Mont-Louis, 1911 ; J. A. de Baïf, *Les Amours de Francine*, édition critique par Ernesta Caldarini, Geneva, Droz ; Paris, Minard, 1966-67, 2 vols. (Textes Littéraires Français).

[3] A. Hulubei, *L'Églogue en France au XVIe siècle*, Paris, Droz, 1938 (on Baïf, see especially pp. 339-56, 368-83, 386-401, 514-9).

[4] W. L. Wiley, " Antoine de Baïf and the Ovidian Love-Tale ", *Studies in Philology*, XXXIII, 1936, pp. 45-54. Forthcoming articles by my colleague, Dr W. G. van Emden, will investigate the debt of Baïf to mediaeval versions of the Pyramus legend.

[5] L. V. Simpson, " Some unrecorded sources of Baïf's *Livre des Météores* ", *Publication of the Modern Language Association* XLVII, December 1932, pp. 1012-27 (Miss Simpson's conclusion that " Aristotle supplies the foundation of Baïf's astronomical system " is disputed by H. Carrington Lancaster, " Baïf and Pontano ", *P.M.L.A.* XLVIII, September 1933, p. 943, on the grounds that she neglects Pontano's role as major source) ; A.-M. Schmidt, *La poésie scientifique en France au XVIe siècle*, Paris, Albin Michel, 1938, pp. 167-76.

[6] M. Morrison, " Catullus and the Poetry of the Renaissance in France ", *Bibliothèque d'Humanisme et Renaissance* XXV, 1963 (" Baïf and Catullus ", pp. 25-46).

[7] M. Raymond, *L'Influence de Ronsard sur la poésie française* (1550-1585), Paris, Champion, 1927, 2 vols. (reprinted 1965 in 1 volume), pp. 132-66 ; also, *Bibliographie Critique de Ronsard en France* (1550-1585), Paris, Champion, 1927, pp. 15-19.

[8] J. Hutton, *The Greek Anthology in France and in the Latin writers of the Netherlands to the year 1800*, Ithaca, New York, Cornell University Press, 1946 (Cornell Studies in Classical Philology, Vol. XXVIII), pp. 47-50, 337-50, 357-61, 368-70.

[9] Dr G. C. Bird has already published the first volume of her projected two volume edition of *Jean-Antoine de Baïf, Chansonnettes*, University of British Columbia, 1964, which contains text, introduction and glossary. Volume II will include a discussion of sources and a critical study.

It is hoped that this present paper will not only discover the sources of certain passages and poems published for the first time in Baïf's collective works, the *Euvres en rime* of 1572-3,[10] but will also reveal interesting insights into some of the techniques and methods he employs in adapting and transposing his Greek, Latin and French models.

In Book I of the *Poemes* there appears a piece entitled *Vie des Chams*, the principal movement of which is a eulogy on the rustic life borrowed, as Augé-Chiquet has noted, from Virgil, *Georgics*, II, ll. 458-540.[11] This eulogy, which begins at line 57 of the poem, has already been the subject of critical examination, and the successful, personal and poetic nature of Baïf's skilful adaptation of Virgil—especially in the familiar and realistic descriptions of the French text—has been discussed.[12] This celebration of rustic life, however, is preceded by an opening movement which contrasts the wretched state of man with the happy lot of the animals and this part of the poem has been neglected :

> Je maudiray la marâtre nature
> De m'avoir fait nêtre en la race dure
> Des maleureux pauvres & foibles hommes,
> Qui plus chetifs que nulle beste sommes.
> La nature a doné dés leur nessance
> Aux animaux leur arme & leur defance :
> Les uns la corne, aucuns ont la vitesse,
> D'autres la pate, & d'autres s'on les blesse
> Frapent des pieds & devant & derriere,
> Aucuns dentuz d'une machoire fiere
> Claquent leurs dents. Ils ont contre l'injure
> Du tems divers une épesse fourure :
> Et sont ils nés ? La plus grande partie
> Trouve à ses pieds de quoy nourrir sa vie.
> Mais las ! tou-nuds & sans armes quelconques
> Nous rechignons en naissant, desadonques

[10] The *Euvres en rime* were published in Paris by Lucas Breyer. The contents of the two volumes were divided into four sections, described on the verso of the frontispiece as : IX livres des Poemes, VII livres des Amours (there are in fact nine books), V livres des Jeux, V livres des Passetems.

[11] *La Vie, les Idées et l'Œuvre de Jean-Antoine de Baïf*, p. 218 and note 5. Marcel Raymond, *Bibliographie Critique de Ronsard en France*, p. 17, suggests a comparison between Baïf's *Vie des Chams* and Ronsard's *Discours à Odet de Coligny*, composed sometime between August 1557 and December 1558 and originally entitled *Elegie a Monseigneur le reverendissime Cardinal de Chatillon* (cf. Ronsard, *Œuvres complètes*, ed. Paul Laumonier, Paris, Société des Textes Français Modernes, 1914-67, 18 vols. : Vol. X, pp. 5-15. For the composition date of this elegy, see Laumonier, loc. cit., p. 7, note 4). Raymond comments that " certains traits viennent probablement de Ronsard " and gives textual references for comparison. His assertions, however, are not supported by a close examination of the passages, for any similarity between the two poems is due to the fact that both are imitated from a common source (Virgil). Moreover, the question of the respective composition dates of the two poems could well argue against Ronsard as a possible influence here (see below, p. 81). Future references to the poetry of Ronsard are given to the Laumonier edition cited above.

[12] M. Augé-Chiquet, op. cit., pp. 227-8 and note 3 ; H. Chamard, *Histoire de la Pléiade*, Paris, Didier, 1939-40, 4 vols. (reprinted 1961-3) : Vol. III, pp. 176-7. Cf. also my edition of Baïf, *Poems*, Oxford, Blackwell's French Texts, 1970, notes to lines 175-180 and 191-8 of *Vie des Chams*.

Montrant sentir par nos cris lamentables
Que nous naissons pour vivre miserables
Humant cet air. La pauvre gent huméne
Ne se nourrit qu'en sueur & qu'en peine.[13]

These lines are clearly a paraphrase of the essential ideas and details of Pliny, *Naturalis Historia*, VII, I, 1-5, and more particularly of the following passage which was frequently adapted by the poets of the Pléiade :[14]

> Principium iure tribuetur homini, cuius causa videtur cuncta alia genuisse natura magna, saeva mercede contra tanta sua munera, ut non sit satis aestimare, parens melior homini an tristior noverca fuerit. ante omnia unum animantium cunctorum alienis velat opibus, ceteris varie tegimenta tribuit, testas, cortices, spinas, coria, villos, saetas, pilos, plunam, pinnas, squamas, vellera ; truncos etiam arboresque cortice, interdum gemino, a frigoribus et calore tutata est : hominem tantum nudum et in nuda humo natali die abicit ad vagitus statim et ploratum, nullumque tot animalium aliud pronius ad lacrimas, et has protinus vitae principio. (loc. cit., 1-2)

The idea that man's tears at birth anticipate a life of misery can be found in several other classical texts[15] and there is some evidence here to suggest a contamination of lines from Lucretius. Pliny does not associate man's weeping with a life of grief except by implication, whereas Lucretius, like Baïf, specifically gives the tears a symbolic force in the following well known passage :

> tum porro puer, ut saevis proiectus ab undis
> navita nudus humi iacet, infans, indigus omni
> vitali auxilio, cum primum in luminis oras
> nixibus ex alvo matris natura profudit,
> vagituque locum lugubri complet, ut aecumst
> cui tantum in vita restet transire malorum.[16]

The French poem continues with a long passage in which Baïf traces man's misery to his reason :

> Nature non ne nous a pas fait étre
> Mieux fortunés pour nous avoir fait nétre
> De la raison ayans l'ame pourvuë,
> Que par trop cher elle nous a venduë.
> Des Animaux la race moins chetive
> Que n'est la nôtre, (à son mal inventive

---

[13] *Euvres en rime de Jan Antoine de Baïf*, ed. Charles Marty-Laveaux, Paris, Lemerre, 1881-90, 5 vols. (Collection de la Pléiade Françoise : reprinted by Slatkine Reprints, Geneva) : Vol. II, pp. 36-7. Subsequent references to Baïf's verse relate to this edition.

[14] Cf. Ronsard, VIII, 188, 187-92 ; IX, 21, 107-22 ; du Bellay, *Œuvres poétiques*, ed. Henri Chamard, Paris, Société des Textes Français Modernes, 1908-31, 6 vols. : IV, 131, 17-32 ; Baïf, II, 405 ; V, 153. The commonplace motif concerning Nature as " mère " or " marâtre ", which originates from the Pliny text, is often referred to in the work of Ronsard (VII, 301-2 ; X, 75, s.X ; X, 310, 47-8 ; X, 368, 101-2), du Bellay (I, 115, s. CIII ; II, 12, s. IX ; II, 86, s. XLV ; *Deffence et Illustration*, Book I, chapter I, opening sentence) and Baïf (IV, 301 ; V, 75).

[15] Apart from the Lucretius text, cf. *The Greek Anthology*, Book X, no. 84 ; Seneca, *Ad Marciam De Consolatione*, XI, 4.

[16] *De Rerum Natura*, V, 222-7. Ronsard frequently recalls this text of Lucretius (cf. VIII, 173, 213-6 ; X, 318, 73-6).

De mille soins) autre soin ne se done
Que l'apetit que sa nature ou bone
Ou bien mauvaise ainsi qu'elle est encline,
Luy a doné : Mais la raison maline
Qui nous gouverne, outre ceux de nature
Dix mille maux encore nous procure.
Nous faisons cas si quelcun eternuë,
Pour un seul mot nous avons l'ame emuë,
Un songe vain en dormant nous effraye,
Nous palissons du cry d'une Frezaye.
Les vains honeurs, les sottes bigotises,
De plus grands biens les palles convoitises,
L'ambition que rien ne ressasie,
Des sens troublez la fausse fantasie,
Et les rigueurs des loix qui nous étonnent,
Ce sont les maux que les homes se donnent
Par leur raison, outre ceux dont leur vie
De sa nature est troublee & suivie.
C'est tout malheur que la vie de l'home,
Que sa raison ronge mine & consome.
En quelque état que le chetif s'employe
L'ennuy le suit : nulle bien nette joye
Il ne reçoit : Mais si l'home peut estre
Heureux, il l'est en la vie champestre.   (II, 37-8)

The central movement of this passage (from " Des Animaux . . ." to
". . . troublee & suivie ") is imitated from a fragment of Menander which
Baïf could have read in Stobaeus, *Florilegium*, section XCVIII, where there
is a collection of extracts from Greek gnomic and elegiac poets centred on
the theme of human grief :

All living beings are most blessed and are possessed of sense much
more than man. For example, take this jackass here. His lot is
luckless, as is generally agreed. For him no evils come through himself, but he has only those which Nature has imposed upon him.
Whereas we, apart from necessary evils, ourselves through ourselves
contrive others in addition. Let someone sneeze and we're perturbed ;
let someone revile us and we're vexed ; if someone sees a vision we
are greatly frightened ; hoots an owl, we are filled with fear. Conten-
tions, reputations, ambitious rivalries, and laws—these evils have all
been added to those that Nature gives.[17]

Although Ronsard paraphrased the same fragment of Menander—together with a piece of Philemon also found in the same section of Stobaeus's
anthology—in an odelette to Jean de Pardaillan Panjas le Jeune of the
Bocage of 1554, there is no evidence here of any inter-influence between the
two French texts. Even supposing Ronsard's poem was available to Baïf
when he composed the *Vie des Chams*,[18] Baïf is clearly following the original
Greek rather than the free paraphrase of his fellow poet which reads :

Mais nous, pauvres chetifs, soit de jour ou de nuit,

[17] *Menander : The principal fragments*, English translation by Francis G. Allinson,
London, Heinemann, 1959 (Loeb Classical Library), p. 483.
[18] On this question of the composition date of *Vie des Chams*, see below p. 81.

> Tousjours quelque tristesse épineuse nous suit,
> Qui nous lime le cœur : si quelcun esternüe
> Nous sommes courroussés : si quelcun par la rüe
> Passe plus grand que nous, nous tressuons d'ahan :
> Si nous oyons crier de nuit quelque Chouan,
> Nous herissons d'effroi : bref, à la race humaine
> Tousjours de quelque part lui survient quelque peine,
> Car il ne lui soufist de ses propres malheurs
> Qu'elle a des le berceau, mais elle en charche ailleurs :
> La court, procés, l'amour, la rancœur, la faintise,
> L'ambition, l'honneur, l'ire, & la convoitise,
> Et le sale appetit d'amonceler des biens
> Sont les maus estrangers que l'homme adjouste aus siens.
>   (VI, 117, 19-32)

Not only does Baïf rigidly reproduce the movement and development of Menander throughout, but he borrows illustrations and details which Ronsard rejects from the Greek fragment (the reference to the frightening vision and to the line " let someone revile us and we're vexed "). Conversely, details peculiar to Ronsard's poem which have no counterpart in Menander (for example the lines,

> . . . . .si quelcun par la rüe
> Passe plus grand que nous, nous tressuons d'ahan,)

are similarly absent in Baïf.

If Ronsard is absent from this particular movement, one is tempted at first glance to see his presence in the opening and closing lines of the extract quoted above, where Baïf expresses the idea that reason is the source of human misery. Neither Pliny nor Menander specifically associates man's suffering with his reason—although it could be said that the Greek text *implies* this idea—but such an association is found on several occasions in the verse of Ronsard and, more especially, in two movements from poems which appeared in his first collective edition of 1560. The first of these is found in the *Epitafe d'André Blondet*.[19] The second passage, from an elegy to Robert de la Haye, is more likely to have had a direct influence on Baïf's poem, for here Ronsard, like his fellow poet, expressly places his criticism of human reason in the context of a comparison with the animals :

> De tous les animaux le plus lourd animal,
> C'est l'homme, le subject d'infortune & de mal,
>
> . . . .
> Toutesfois à l'ouir discrettement parler,
> Vous diriés que soubdain au ciel il doit voller,
> Tant il faict en parlant de la beste entendue,
> Ignorant que les dieux luy ont trop cher vendue
> Cette pauvre raison, qui malheureux le fait,
> D'autant que par sus tous il s'estime parfaict.
>
> . . . .
> Et pour trop raisonner miserable il demeure,
> Sans se pouvoir garder qu'à la fin il ne meure :

[19] X, 309-10, 23-38.

Au contraire les cerfs qui n'ont point de raison,
Les poissons, les oiseaux, sont dans comparaison
Trop plus heureux que nous, qui sans soing & sans peine
Errent de tous costez où le plaisir les meine.

(X, 316-7, ll. 31-2, 39-44, 53-8)

What seems to confirm an inter-influence between Ronsard and Baïf here, however, is not merely the similarity of interpretation concerning animal superiority, human misery and reason—this, after all, is a commonplace of sceptical dialectic[20]—but rather the textual parallel between Baïf's couplet,

De la raison ayans l'ame pourvuë,
Que par trop cher elle nous a venduë,

and the following lines from either Ronsard's epitaph to Blondet,

Mais par sur tous l'homme, qui est semblable
D'esprit aux dieux, est le plus miserable,
Et la raison qui vient divinement
Luy est vendue un peu trop cherement :

(X, 309, 23-6)

or from the elegy to Robert de la Haye,

Ignorant que les dieux luy ont trop cher vendue
Cette pauvre raison, qui malheureux le fait.

(X, 317, 42-3)

However, such reasoning assumes that Baïf's *Vie des Chams* was composed after 1560, which is by no means certain. Although there is no internal evidence to suggest a composition date, Augé-Chiquet is of the opinion that Baïf wrote the *Vie des Chams* before 1552 and that it was " parmi ses toutes premières œuvres ".[21] His arguments are based on the fact that Baïf uses the decasyllabic line and exclusively feminine rhymes throughout his poem, whereas after 1552 he seriously began alternating masculine and feminine rhymes and showed a developing preference for the alexandrine line. If we accept the reasoning of Augé-Chiquet concerning the composition date of the *Vie des Chams*, then we are obliged to conclude that it is Ronsard who owes a textual debt to Baïf in the above lines.[22]

Baïf, incidentally, is not consistent in his scepticism, and a totally different attitude to human reason than that expressed in the *Vie des Chams* or that attributed to him in the *Dialogues* of Guy de Brués is found in a piece dedicated *A Nicolas Nicolai*[23] of the fourth book of *Poemes* :

[20] It is worth while noting that the same sceptical arguments are attributed to Baïf in the first dialogue of *Les Dialogues contre les Nouveaux Academiciens* of Guy de Brués (1557).

[21] Op. cit., p. 276. Cf. also, p. 268.

[22] It could justifiably be argued that it is somewhat dangerous to establish a composition date purely on the evidence of matters of versification. Augé-Chiquet is certainly wrong when he dates the composition of *Les Muses* (II, 71-91) as pre-1552 because of the use of the decasyllabic line (op. cit., p. 268) as I have demonstrated in my edition of Baïf, *Poems* (see notes to poem no. XXVIII).

[23] Nicolas de Nicolaï, seigneur d'Arfeuille, was a traveller and geographer who published his *Quatre premiers livres des Navigations et Peregrinations Orientales* in 1568 (Lyon, G. Roville). Ronsard wrote a prefatory poem to this work (XV, 371-5) but there is no evidence of any inter-influence between Ronsard's elegy and Baïf's piece.

Mais je ne puis que je ne m'esmerveille
Considerant cette ame nompareille
Qui de tant d'arts nous a fait ouverture
En renforçant nostre foible nature.
Lon a domté mainte beste farouche :
Mettant à l'une un mors dedans la bouche,
A l'autre on a sous le joug qu'elle porte
Lié le front d'une courroye forte :
L'une nous sert en tems de paix & guerre,
L'autre d'un soc ouvre la bonne terre :
Lon a trouvé le soigneux labourage,
Et du fourment & des vignes l'usage :
Lon a cherché dans le terrestre ventre
Le dur acier. Dessus la mer on entre
Dans les vaisseaux : & à rame ou à voile
Lon vogue ayant l'œil fiché sur l'etoile
S'il fait serein : s'il fait nuble, en la carte
Par le quadran lon voit si on s'écarte.   (II, 206)

The general idea that man's reason (Baïf's " ame nompareille " is the equivalent of reason) has elevated him above the animals and given him mastery over the physical and natural world is suggested here by a famous passage from Manilius, *Astronomicon*, IV, ll. 875-902, a text which du Bellay translated for Louis Le Roy's French commentary on Plato's *Symposium* (1558).[24] Apart from the general theme Manilius provides Baïf with the specific examples of man's domination over the land, sea and animals in a series of brief references which the French poet develops at greater length :

unius inspectus rerum viresque loquendi
ingeniumque capax ; variasque educitur artis
hic partus, qui cuncta regit : secessit in urbis,
edomuit terram ad fruges, animalia cepit
imposuitque viam ponto.[25]

★   ★   ★

If the *Vie des Chams* revealed a complex interweaving of reminiscences from Pliny, Menander, Lucretius, Ronsard (?) and Virgil, it is Menander alone who reappears as source of a piece from Book VII of the *Poemes* entitled *A Monsieur de Mauru* :

MAURU, si quelque Promethee
Avec la puissance arrestee
Par le conseil du touts les Dieux,
De tels mots venoit me poursuivre :
Quand seras mort te faut revivre :
Il est conclu dedans les cieux.
Et quand tu viendras à renaistre
Tu seras lequel voudras estre,
Bouc, ou Belier, ou chat, ou chien,

[24] Du Bellay, ed. cit., VI, 440-2.
[25] Loc. cit., ll. 893-7. L. V. Simpson, art. cit., pp. 1013-5, suggests Manilius as a source for certain lines of *Le Premier des Meteores* devoted to the Milky Way.

Homme, ou cheval, ou autre beste.
Choisi-la sans plus & l'arreste :
Et tel que tu voudras revien.
Tu n'en pourras estre delivre :
Car derechef il te faut vivre :
C'est du destin la dure loy.
Choisi donc ce que tu veux estre.
Ma foy je luy diroy, Mon Maistre,
Tout, pourveu qu'homme je ne soy :
Car de tous les animaux l'homme
Est le plus miserable, comme
Tu l'entendras par mes raisons.
Plus injustement il se tréte
Que nulle beste à luy sugéte,
Maleureux en toutes saisons.
Le Cheval le meilleur on pense
Avecque soing & diligence
Plustost que celuy qui moins vaut.
On l'epoussette, on le bouchonne :
Avéne foin paille on luy donne :
Et jamais rien ne luy defaut.
Si fusses un bon chien de chasse,
D'un Seigneur tu aurois la grace,
Qui t'estimant t'honoreroit
Plus qu'un autre qui seroit pire :
Et sçachant ta valeur élire,
Hors du chenil te tireroit.
Un coc s'il a de l'excellance
De sa race ou de sa vaillance,
Est mieux qu'un lâche coc traité,
Que lon egorge ou que lon donne.
Au bon la Court on abandonne,
Où l'orge à plein poing est jetté.
Mais l'homme tant bon qu'il puisse estre,
Sage, vaillant, sçavant, adestre,
Pour cela n'est plus haut monté.
Car soudain sur luy court l'envie :
Et traisnant sa maudite vie
Gist par sa vertu rebouté.
Un flateur davant touts se pousse,
Qui traistre de sa bouche douce
Pipe par un langage doux.
Le Medisant apres s'avance.
Un bon artisan de mechance
Se fait rechercher entre touts.
J'aime donc mieux, s'il faut revivre,
Estre asne, que d'avoir à vivre
Homme, dont la vertu n'a pris :
Pour voir davant mes yeux le pire
Avoir tous les biens qu'il desire,
Et le meilleur vivre à mépris.   (II, 366-8)

The structure and development of ideas, the examples of the horse, dog
and cock and the accompanying moral and satirical commentary are all

closely imitated from a fragment of Menander preserved in Stobaeus, *Flori-legium*, section CVI, and given below in a Latin translation :

Si quis Deorum jam mihi dicat, Crato,
Ubi vitam functus fueris vives denuo,
Et fies quidvis, hircus, aut canis, aut ovis,
Equus, homo denique : nam revivendum tibi est :
Ita fata sciscunt. opta quam vitam velis :
Dicturus videor illico, fac me quidlibet
Dum ne hominem facias. unum id animantum omnium
Sine merito habet fortunam aut infortunium.
Equorum ut quisque fortis est, curatius
Habetur alio. velox in pretio canis
Majore est, quam projectus ingluvie atque iners.
Generosus fruitur gallus praecipua dape,
Atque ultro ignavus alter potiorem timet.
Homo si quis est bene natus, eductus probe,
Caste moratus, nullum pretium hoc seculo est.
Primas in vita habet assentator, alteras
Calumniator ; at malignus tertias.
Quanto asinum fieri satius quam intuerier
Peiores se pollucibilius vivere !26

Ronsard also used the same Greek fragment in the opening movement of his elegy to Robert de la Haye of 1560,[27] but there is no evidence here of any inter-influence between the two French texts. Unlike Baïf, Ronsard rejects Menander's illustrations for his own examples of a bird, fish and deer ; he also ignores the moral and satirical commentary and in fact borrows little beyond the general idea of being reborn and of preferring to be an animal rather than a man.

★   ★   ★

The opening piece of Book V of the *Poemes* is a *Hymne de la Paix* composed for the marriage between the Protestant Henri de Bourbon, later Henri IV of France, and Marguerite de Valois, daughter of Henri II, which took place on August 18th 1572. Whilst poems celebrating peace were part of the courtier function of the poet and frequently contained stylised themes and commonplace formulae, dictated both by the circumstantial nature of the inspiration and by the convention of the genre itself,[28] the plan of Baïf's " hymne ", the development of its ideas and principal movements as well as certain textual parallels, reveal specific debts to Tibullus, I, x, and, more especially, to an assimilation of four texts of Ronsard on a similar subject :

[26] *Dicta poetarum quae apud Io. Stobaeum exstant. Emendata et latino carmine reddita ab Hugone Grotio*, Paris, Buon, 1623, pp. 442-4. An English translation of the passage can be found in J. M. Edmonds, *The Fragments of Attic Comedy*, Leiden, E. J. Brill, 1961 : Vol. IIIB, pp. 1109-11.

[27] X, 315-6, 1-30.

[28] Cf. for example, Jacques Grévin, *Chant de joie de la paix* ; M. Claude de Buttet, *Hymne à la Paix* ; Rémy Belleau, *Chant de la Paix* (in *Première Journée de la Bergerie*) ; Jean Passerat, *Hymne de la Paix* ; Louis le Roy, *De Pace* ; Jean Dorat, *Neuf cantiques ou sonetz de la Paix* ; du Bellay, *Discours au Roy sur la trefve de l'an M.D.L.V.*

the *Ode de la Paix* (1550), the *Exhortation pour la Paix* (1558), *La Paix, au Roy* (1559) and the *Chant de Liesse, au Roy* (1559).[29]

Whilst Marcel Raymond has remarked that Baïf's " *Hymne de la Paix* fait d'abord songer aux poèmes de circonstance que Ronsard composa en 1559 pour fêter la fin des hostilités ",[30] he has not demonstrated the extent of the influence or suggested specific points of textual similarity or sympathy. Such an exercise is rewarding not only because it will establish the precise areas and the exact nature of the imitation, but also because it will provide an interesting example of a technique of source adaptation and composition where Baïf is at his most successful.

Like Ronsard in his *Ode de la Paix* and *La Paix*, Baïf opens his poem with a dedication in the form of a eulogy,[31] but it is not until the second movement devoted to the cosmic function of Friendship (the daughter of Peace in Baïf's " hymne ") that the similarities become more apparent and more textually significant :

> JE VEU louer la PAIX : c'est la Paix que je chante,
> La fille d'amitié dessur tout excellante.
> Amitié nourrit tout : tout vit par amitié,
> Et rien ne peut mourir que par inimitié.
> La concorde & l'amour sont l'apuy de la vie,
> Et l'effroyable mort vient de haine & d'envie.
> Le ciel, la terre, l'air, & la mer & le feu,
> Et tout le monde entier, d'un amiable neu
> S'entretienent conjoints. Cette belle machine
> Sans la bonne amitié tomberoit en ruine.
> Car, s'ils n'estoyent liez de liaisons d'émant,
> On verroit rebeller tout mutin element,
> Et guerroyer l'un l'autre : & soudain toutes choses
> Dans l'ancien chaôs retomberoyent encloses.   (II, 224)

The idea that Love or Friendship created the world from a chaos of warring elements and continues to preserve it in order and harmony has its origin in Plato's *Timaeus*[32] and *Symposium*. This theme is developed in certain neo-Platonic commentaries, especially that of Marsilio Ficino on the *Symposium* for whom Love is the author, teacher and preserver of the universe :

> Quinetiam unitate partium suarum cuncta servantur, dispersione partium pereunt. Unitatem vero partium mutuus earundem efficit amor. Quod in humoribus nostrorum corporum et mundi elementis intueri licet, quorum concordia, ut ait Empedocles Pythagoreus, et mundus et corpus nostrum consta, discordia dissipatur. Concordiam vero illis pacis atque amoris praestat vicissitudo.

[29] Ronsard, III, 3-35 ; IX, 15-26 ; 103-116 ; 131-141.

[30] *Influence de Ronsard*, I, p. 155, note 3.

[31] Cf. Ronsard, III, 3-5, 1-36 ; IX, 103-6, 1-42 ; and Baïf, II, 223-4.

[32] Op. cit., 29A-31A. This explanation of the creation of the universe is something of a commonplace in both classical philosophy and literature (cf. especially Ovid, *Metamorphoses*, I, l. 5 ff.). For a wealth of references to this theme in the verse of the Pléiade, see R. V. Merrill and R. J. Clements, *Platonism in French Renaissance Poetry*, New York University Press, 1957, pp. 1-28.

. . . .
quamobrem omnes mundi partes, quia unius artificis opera sunt,
eiusdem machinae membra inter se in essendo et vivendo similia,
mutua quadam caritate sibi invicem vinciuntur, ut merito dici possit
amor nodus perpetuus, et copula mundi, partiumque eius immobile
sustentaculum, ac firmum totius machinae fundamentum.[33]

Baïf's notion that " Amitié ", the principle of order, presides over preservation whilst " inimitié ", the principle of discord, causes corruption, is
very close to the conception of Empedocles as defined not only in the passage
from Ficino, quoted above, but also in the following lines from Pontus de
Tyard's *Le Premier Curieux* :

> Et semble qu'Aristote en quelque partie, sinon en tout, ait receu
> l'opinion de l'amitié et discorde d'Empedocle. Comme si la discorde
> signifioit la contrarieté des qualitez, cause de la corruption ; et l'amitié
> ou concorde, la cause de la generation.[34]

Although Baïf may owe a debt to the philosophical ideas of Empedocles
and of Ficino's commentary on Plato's *Symposium* for his definition of the
cosmic role of Amitié, Ronsard's influence in this movement cannot be ruled
out, for his example appears to have contributed to the selection and interpretation of Baïf's material in this instance. In the *Ode de la Paix*, the
Exhortation pour la Paix and *La Paix*, Ronsard describes the cosmic function
of Peace[35] in terms not dissimilar to those of Baïf. Indeed, not only are
there references to the pacification of the original chaos of elements and to
the role of Peace in the preservation of cosmic order in these poems,[36] but
in the following passage from *La Paix* Ronsard's definition of life and death
and his conception of the universe in terms of the antithetical struggle
between " amitié " and " hayne ", harmony and discord, are reminiscent
not only of Empedocles' ideas but are textually close to the Baïf passage
quoted above :

> . . . les astres du ciel, & tout ce qui habite
> D'écaillé dans la mer, les grans monstres des eaux,
> Tout ce qui vit en terre, & les legers oiseaux
> Qui pendus dedans l'air sur les vens se soutiennent
> Sont tous remplis d'amour, & par luy s'entretiennent ?
> Quand pour trop abonder, les elemens divers
> L'un à l'autre ont discord, tout ce grand Univers
> Languist en maladie, & nous montre par signe
> Qu'une hayne nouvelle offence la machine,
> Car l'air qui la reçoit comme subtil et prompt
> Se deult de telle hayne, & soudain se corrompt,

---

[33] *Marsilio Ficino's Commentary on Plato's " Symposium "*, translated and edited
by S. R. Jayne, Columbia, University of Missouri Studies, Vol. XIX, no. I, 1944, pp.
54, 56. In his German translation of Ficino's commentary (*Marsilius Ficinus über
die Liebe oder Platons Gastmahl*, Leipzig, 1914, p. 233, note 4) Karl Hasse suggests that
Ficino's mistake in referring to Empedocles as a Pythagorean is due to Empedocles's
theory of the wandering of the soul.

[34] *The Universe of Pontus de Tyard*, ed. J. Lapp, Cornell University Press, 1950, p. 57.

[35] The substitution of Peace for " Amitié " as the harmonising divinity is explained
by reference to Claudianus, *De consulatu Stilichonis*, II, 6-11.

[36] Ronsard, III, 5-7, 37-68 ; 24-5, 319-24 ; IX, 25, 195-99 ; 107-8, 53-78.

. . . .
Ainsi quand les humeurs qui nostre corps composent
En tranquille amitié dedans nous ne reposent,
Mais en se hayssant, abondent en Discord :
Lors vient la maladie, & bien souvent la mort,[37]

. . . .
Ainsi par l'amitié la vie s'entretient,
Et la mauvaise mort par la noise survient :
Or' voila donc combien la Paix est trop plus belle
Et meilleure aux humains que n'est pas la querelle.[38]

Similarly Baïf's reference to the elements as being "liez de liaisons d'émant" may well be a verbal echo of lines from Ronsard's *Ode de la Paix* of 1550, for although Plato talks of men's bodies being compounded of the elements and being joined together "with numerous small invisible pegs"[39] and although Pindar and Horace refer respectively to "strong bolts of adamant" and "adamantinos . . . clavos",[40] it is Ronsard alone who specifically uses the expression within a context remarkably similar to that of Baïf :

> Puis demembrant l'univers
> En quatre quartiers divers,
> Sa main divinement sainte
> Les lia de clous d'aimant,
> Afin de s'aller aimant
> D'une paisible contrainte.   (III, 6, 45-50)

The third movement of Baïf's poem (ll. 65-88) centres around the theme of the benefits of peace and it is here that textual reminiscences from Ronsard become more emphatic and numerous :

> O qu'on deût bien cherir la Paix toute divine,
> La fille d'Amitié sur toutes choses dine !
> Tout bien & tout plaisir par ses graces fleurît :
> Les arts sont en honneur : la vertu se nourrît,
> Le vice est amorty. Lors sans peur de domage,
> De meurdre & de danger le marchand fait voyage :
> Alors le laboureur au labeur prend plaisir
> Quand le champ non ingrant répond à son désir.
> L'ennemy fourageur son bestial n'emmene,
> Et pillant ne ravît le doux fruit de sa péne :
> Le vin est à qui fait des vignes la façon,
> Et qui fait la semaille en leve la moisson.
> Et Ceres & Bacchus & Palés & Pomone
> Font que parmy les chams grande planté foisone

[37] The first five lines of the extract recall the invocation to Venus which opens Lucretius, *De Rerum Natura*, Book I. The association of the humours of the body and the elements of the universe (ll. 12-15 of the quotation) is in Plato, *Timaeus*, 43A, but Ronsard is much closer here to the Ficino passage cited above.

[38] IX, 112-3, 178-88, 193-6, 199-202. Apart from the more obvious textual parallels it is possible that Ronsard's reference to the world as "la machine" (l. 186) prompted Baïf's "cette belle machine" (l. 9 of passage quoted above). Cf. also, Ronsard, III, 24, 320 ; IX, 108, 73.

[39] *Timaeus*, 43A.

[40] Pindar, *Pythian Odes*, IV, l. 71 ; Horace, *Odes*, III, xxiv, 5-7.

De fruits & de betail. Par tout regne le jeu,
Et le gentil Amour chaufe tout de son feu.
Par tout roullent les fruits du plein cor d'abondance :
Sous l'ombrage lon voit s'egaïer en la dance,
Trepignant pellemelle & fille & garçons,
Tantost au flageolet & tantost aux chansons,
Quand Saturne fut Roy sous une saison telle
La Paix avoit son regne, & le nom de querelle
Pour lors n'etoit conu : ny l'homicide fer
N'avoit esté tiré des abysmes d'enfer.   (II, 225-6)

The general idea of this passage may have been suggested by Tibullus,
1, x, 45-54 :

interea pax arva colat. pax candida primum
    duxit araturos sub iuga curva boves ;
pax aluit vites et sucos condidit uvae,
    funderet ut nato testa paterna merum ;
pace bidens vomerque nitent, at tristia duri
    militis in tenebris occupat arma situs.—
rusticus e lucoque vehit, male sobrius ipse,
    uxorem plaustro progeniemque domum.—
sed veneris tunc bella calent, scissosque capillos
    femina, perfractas conqueriturque fores.

However, two movements from Ronsard's *Exhortation pour la Paix* and
La Paix provide closer parallels with the lines from Baïf's " hymne ".
Especially significant is the following passage from *La Paix* :

Adonques en repos les campaignes jaunissent,
Toutes pleines d'espis, les fleurs s'epanouissent
Le long d'un bas rivage, & plus haut les raisins
Aux sommetz des coutaux nous meurissent leurs vins.
Le peuple à l'aise dort, les citez sont tranquilles,
Les Muses & les ars fleurissent par les villes,
La gravité se montre avecques la vertu,
Et par la sainte loy le vice est abatu,
Les navires sans peur dans les havres abordent,
. . . .
Venus avec son filz (elle de ses flameches,
Luy enfant tout armé de trousses & de fleches)
Errent parmi le peuple, & aux jeunes plaisirs
Des combas amoureux chatouillent noz desirs :
Amour comme une flamme entre dans noz courages,
Il assemble les cœurs, il joinct les mariages,
Fait dances & festins, et en lieu de tuer
Les humains, comme Mars, les fait perpetuer.
On ne s'eveille point aux effrois des allarmes,
Le dos n'est point courbé soubs la charge des armes,
On n'oit plus les canons horriblement tonner,
Mais la lyre & le luth doucement resonner
Aupres de sa maistresse, & se nourir l'oreille
Du son, & la baiser en la bouche vermeille.
. . . .
On chante, on saute, on rid par les belles preries,

On fait tournois, festins, masques, & mommeries,
Chacun vit sans contrainte & à son aise aussi,
Et du pied contre terre on foulle le soucy.
(IX, 111-112, 141-9, 153-66, 173-6)

A comparison of this passage with that of Baïf reveals similarities not
only of theme but of treatment and details of expression. For example, the
references to the flourishing of the arts, the appearance of virtue and the
suppression of vice in times of peace, whilst absent in Tibullus, are nevertheless present in the same order in both Ronsard and Baïf. Likewise both
French texts mention the safe passage of shipping, an idea not found in the
Latin text. Again, although Tibullus briefly associates Love and Peace in I,
x, 53, and although his evocation of the Elysian fields in I, iii,

hic choreae cantusque vigent, ...
. . . .
ac iuvenum series teneris immixta puellis
ludit, et adsidue proelia miscet amor,[41]

could have suggested the odd detail to Baïf, the entire description of Love's
sport, with allusions to dancing, music and merriment, is close to the Ronsard
text.[42]

With the mention of the benefits of peace to farming, agriculture and
viniculture, Baïf is contaminating his recollection of the passage from *La
Paix*, quoted above, with reminiscences from lines of Ronsard's *Exhortation
pour la Paix* : certainly his reference to the horticultural divinities Ceres,
Bacchus, Pales and Pomone, as well as his brief allusion to the abundance
of fruit, echo the following passage from Ronsard's 1558 poem :

La paix fertilisa les campaignes steriles,
La paix de soubs le joug fist mugir les toreaux,
La paix dedans les prez fist sauter les troupeaux,
La paix sur les coutaux tira droit à la ligne
Les ordres arengez de la premiere vigne :
De raisins empamprez Bacche elle environna,
Et le chef de Ceres de fourment couronna,
Elle enfla tout le sein de la belle Pomonne
D'abondance de fruitz que nous produit l'Autonne.[43]

In the same way the development of ideas in Ronsard's *Exhortation* may
provide a clue to Baïf's association of his account of the benefits of peace
with the reign of Saturn and the Golden Age myth. It is true, of course,
that the reign of Peace is closely linked with the Age of Gold—without
necessarily being identical with it—in Ancient, Medieval and Renaissance
literature,[44] and the commonplaceness of the theme and the brevity of
Baïf's allusion make it doubly difficult to establish a definite source for the

[41] Loc. cit., ll. 59, 63-4.

[42] Cf. similar references to love, dancing and youthful sport in times of peace in
the *Ode de la Paix* (III, 25-6, 343-6).

[43] IX, 25, 200-8. There is perhaps a recollection of Tibullus, I, x, 68 (" profluat et
pomis candidus ante sinus ") in the last two lines of this passage.

[44] On this point, consult Elizabeth Armstrong, *Ronsard and the Age of Gold*, Cambridge University Press, 1968, passim.

last four lines of the movement. The negative structure of the verse suggests
Tibullus, 1, iii, 35, 47-8, as a likely influence,

> quam bene Saturno vivebant rege, . . .
> . . . .
> non acies, non ira fuit, non bella, nec ensem
> immiti saevus duxerat arte faber.

but within the context of so many Ronsardian echoes it is conceivable that
Baïf's selection and development of material at this stage may owe a debt
to two consecutive movements from the *Exhortation*, the first of which
evokes the Age of Iron[45] and curses,

> . . . . celuy qui dechira la terre,
> Et dedans ses boyaux le fer y alla querre,[46]

the second of which refers to the Age of Gold :

> Qu'heureuse fut la gent qui vivoit sous Saturne,
> Quand l'aise & le repos, & la paix taciturne,
> Bien loing de la trompette, & bien loing des soldars,
> Loing du fer & de l'or, erroit de toutes pars
> Par les bois assurée, & du fruit de la terre
> En commun se paissoit sans fraude ny sans guerre.[47]

What makes an influence more probable at this stage is that Baïf continues to construct the major themes of his " hymne " along the lines of
the *Exhortation*. Like Ronsard in his poem, Baïf follows his allusion to the
Age of Gold with a movement devoted to an account of the horrors of war,[48]
the second half of which reads :

> O la pitié de voir la flamme qui sacage
> Devorant sans mercy les maisons d'un vilage !
> De voir dans le faubourg le pauvre citoyen
> Qui ne pardonne pas au logis qui est sien !
> O la pitié de voir les meres desolees,
> De leurs piteux enfans tendrement acolees,
> S'en aler d'huis en huis leur vie quemander,
> A qui bien peu devant lon souloit demander !
> O la pitié de voir labourer une ville !
> O la pitié de voir la campagne fertile
> Faite un hideux desert ! O pitié, mais horreur
> De voir l'exploit cruel d'une chaude fureur !
> De voir en sens rassis un horrible carnage
> De morts & demi-morts cacher un labourage :
> Ouir les tristes cris : Voir hommes & chevaux
> Pesle-mesle entassez : Voir de sang les ruisseaux !
> (II, 226-7)

Although there is some evidence of textual sympathy in this movement
between the *Exhortation pour la Paix* and Baïf's " hymne " which goes

---

[45] IX, 21-2, 123-46.

[46] Loc. cit., ll. 123-4.

[47] IX, 23, 147-52. Cf. the same association of the coming of peace with the Golden
Age in Ronsard's *Chant de Liesse* (IX, 132, l. 15 ff.).

[48] Cf. Baïf, II, 226-7, and Ronsard, IX, 23-4, 157-70. See also Ronsard's *La Paix*
(IX, 109-110, 107-40).

beyond mere similarity of general theme and development of ideas,[49] the major inspiration is clearly the following passage of Ronsard's *Chant de Liesse* :

> Quel plaisir est-ce en lieu d'ouyr les armes,
> De voir les champs tous foullez de gendarmes,
> De voyr en l'air les estendars rempans
> En taffetas, tout ainsy que serpens
> Qui vont par l'herbe, & d'un col qui menace
> A cent repliz entre-coupent leur trace ?
> De voyr le fer des souldars tous sanglans,
> Voyr les vieillardz tous palles & tremblans,
> Mourir de coups aupres de leur famille ?
> Voyr une mere, une veufve, une fille
> Porter au col ou son frere ou son filz,
> Et pauvrement mandier d'huys en huys ?
> Quel plaisir est-ce en lieu de voyr les villes,
> Places, chasteaux, & campaignes fertilles
> De haut en bas & razer & brusler,
> Et jusqu'au ciel les plaintes se mesler
> D'hommes, d'enfans, de filles & de femmes,
> Sauvant leurs corps demy brullez de flammes ?
> Quel plaisir est-ce, en lieu d'ouyr le bruit
> D'un mur tombé, ou d'un rampar destruit,
> Voyr maintenant à Paris dans les rues,
> De tes sujectz les troupes espendues
> Joyeusement à ce retour de l'an
> Crier Hyman ô Hymené, Hyman,
> Verser œilletz & liz, comme une pluye
> Tombe en esté quand le chaut nous ennuye ?
>   (IX, 133-4, 35-60)

Baïf's debt to Ronsard is seen here not only in the details of the evocation of the havoc and horrors of war, but also in the borrowing of a repetitive structure and refrain (Ronsard, " Quel plaisir . . . de voir " ; Baïf, " O la pitié de voir ") and in certain verbal reminiscences.[50] At the same time it is interesting to note that the process of contaminating Ronsard's poems celebrating peace extends backwards to the lines from Baïf's " hymne " which immediately precede the extract last quoted, for these lines, which introduce the theme of the horrors of war,

> L'ambition des grands & la gloute avarice
> Font qu'ils tentent les Rois de rancueur animez,

---

[49] The last six lines of the extract from Baïf quoted above are similar in certain details—the piles of dead men and horses and the blood-red waters—to lines 157-162 of Ronsard's *Exhortation* :

> Las ! je ne verrois point tant de glaives tranchans,
> Tant de monceaux de mors qui engressent les champs,
> Tant de chevaux occis dechargez de leur somme
> Empescher tout le cours de Moselle ou de Somme,
> Ny tant de mourions, ny de plastrons ferrez,
> Tenir les rouges flotz de la Meuse enserrez.

[50] Lines 5-7 of the Baïf extract are very close to lines 10-12 of the Ronsard quotation. Cf. also Baïf's " campagne fertile " (l. 10) and Ronsard's " campaignes fertilles " (l. 14) and the identical rhymes of Baïf, ll. 9-10 and Ronsard, ll. 13-14.

Pour se trouver aux chams camp contre camp armez.
Là le premier armé la ville forte assiege :
L'autre hatif apres vient pour lever le siege,
Ou s'il ne vient à tems d'assaut la ville on prend,
Ou ne pouvant tenir sans force elle se rend.
Apres le pauvre peuple & la foible vieillesse
Les femmes & l'enfance en cris & larmes lesse
Son païs sacagé. L'injurieux soudard
Ravît le saint honeur aux filles sans égard.   (II, 226)

appear to recall this extract from Ronsard's *La Paix* :

Un peuple contre l'autre en armes se remue,
Une forte cité contre l'autre est esmue,
Un prince contre l'autre ordonne son arroy,
Et un Roy dans son camp deffie un autre Roy.
. . . .
. . . . la cruelle arrogance
Du fer ambitieux se donne la licence
De vaguer impunie, & sans avoir egard
A la crainte des loix, perse de part en part
Aussi bien l'estomac d'une jeune pucelle,
Que celuy d'un enfant qui pend à la mamelle,
Les vieillars de leurs litz tremblans sont deboutez,
Et l'image de mort paroist de tous costez.[51]

After his evocation of the destruction of war, Baïf's fifth movement is centred around a meditation on the misery and fragility of the human condition :

Et quel plaisir prens-tu, race frelle chetive,
De te hâter la mort, qui jamais n'est tardive,
Sinon qu'en te donnant mille maux ennuieux
Tu fais le vivre tel que le mourir vaut mieux ?
Ta sote outrecuidance & ta folle avarice
Redouble ton malheur faisant de vertu vice.
O de la bonne terre inutile fardeau,
(Qui dois en peu de jours geté sous le tumbeau
Aviander les vers) tu partroubles ta vie
De vaine inimitié de tant de maux suivie.
Que veux-tu conquester ? Je croy tu te promês
En ce monde incertain une vie à jamês.
Aveugle ouvre tes yeux : Regarde miserable
Que ta condition est pauvre & peu durable.
Où vont les plus grands Rois & plus grands Empereurs ?
Mais que sont aujourdhuy les plus grands conquereurs ?
Qui par force ont donté, rangeans sous leur puissance
Les trois parts de la terre en serve obeïssance ?
Ils ne sont plus que poudre, & n'en reste sinon,
(Si nous en reste rien) que le son de leur nom,
Qu'ils ont voulu nommer la bonne renommee,
Qui n'est apres la mort qu'une ombre de fumee.

(II, 227)

[51] Loc. cit., ll. 109-112, 125-132. Similar reference to the slaughtering of the aged and the raping of women in the *Exhortation* (l. 168).

Whilst Baïf's opening words (" Et quel plaisir . . .") are a reminiscence of the same passage of Ronsard's *Chant de Liesse* which had inspired the previous movement of the " hymne ",[52] the theme and interrogative structure of the first four lines appear to be modelled more closely on Tibullus, 1, x, 33-4 :

> quis furor est atram bellis accersere Mortem ?
> imminet et tacito clam venit illa pede.

Baïf's debt to the Latin text may, however, be indirect in this instance, for he may well have passed through the intermediary of the following lines of Ronsard's *Exhortation pour la Paix*, the movement and content of which are adapted from Tibullus :

> Quelle fureur vous tient de vous entretuer,
> Et devant vostre temps aux Enfers vous ruer,
> A grans coups de cannons, de piques & de lance ?
> La mort vient assez tost, helas ! sans qu'on l'avance,
> Et de cent millions qui vivent en ce temps,
> Un à peine vient-il au terme de cent ans.
>
> (loc. cit., ll. 81-6)

There is a piece of evidence—apart from Baïf's constant recollection of Ronsard's *Exhortation* elsewhere in the " hymne "—to suggest that Baïf's debt is more directly to this text of Ronsard than to Tibullus. In line 7 of the extract quoted above, Baïf refers to the human race as " de la bonne terre inutile fardeau " and this allusion echoes a detail of a myth developed in a passage of the *Exhortation* which immediately follows the lines last quoted. In this passage Ronsard addresses the earth and, in a variant of line 93 of the 1567-87 editions of the poem, specifically refers to mankind as a " fardeau " :

> On dit que quelquefoys te sentant trop chargée
> D'hommes qui te foulloyent, pour estre soulagée
> Du fardeau qui pressoit ton echine si fort
> Tu prias Jupiter de te donner confort.[53]

Similarly, considering the frequent recollections of Ronsard throughout Baïf's " hymne ", the latter may well be indebted to his fellow poet for the ideas of the omnipotence of death and the fragility of fame which close the movement. Whilst these themes are literary commonplaces found especially in Pindar and Horace,[54] Ronsard, unlike either of the classical poets, had expressed these ideas in *La Paix* of 1559 in precisely the same context as Baïf, namely to reinforce his arguments against war and to underline his moral advice to the king :

[52] The refrain " Quel plaisir de voir . . . d'ouyr " appears in lines 35, 47, 53, 61, 73, 85 of the *Chant de Liesse*.

[53] IX, 20, 91-4 (text quoted is that of the 1567 edition). The legend, recounted in lines 91-106, tells how " la méchante Discorde " was sent to alleviate the burden of mankind on the earth.

[54] Pindar, *Nemean*, VII, epode 1 and antistr. 2 ; Horace, *Odes*, I, iv, 13-15 ; xxviii ; II, iii, 21-8 ; xvi, 29-30 ; xviii.

Pensez vous estre Dieu, l'honneur du monde passe,
Il faut un jour mourir quelque chose qu'on face,
Et apres vostre mort, fussiez vous Empereur,
Vous ne serez non plus qu'un simple laboureur.

(IX, 114-5, 233-6)

The next movement of Baïf's " hymne " takes the form of general moral maxims offered to " qui veut en ce monde un bon bruit aquerir " and, more particularly, of advice to the king. Whilst of course such moral instruction is part of a humanist and Christian tradition, it is of interest to note that Ronsard also includes similar passages of moral commonplaces in his *Ode de la Paix* and *La Paix*.[55] Although there are no direct textual echoes from Ronsard's poems at this stage, this similarity of theme is further evidence that Baïf appears to be modelling the overall plan and development of his material on an assimilation of Ronsard's peace poems.

The final movement of Baïf's poem (lines 173-212) provides further proof of his debt to Ronsard concerning the general composition and structure of his themes, for like his fellow-poet in *La Paix*, Baïf puts his moral advice to the king in the context of a plea for Christian unity :[56]

Non le dur Canibal, non le More Barbare,
Non l'infidele Turc, non le vagant Tartare,
Il a fait vos sugets : Il vous soumét les siens,
Nous, qui de Christ son fils avons nom Chrestiens :
Nous qui sommes lavés de l'eau du saint Battesme :
Nous qui sommes sacrés & croizés du saint Cresme :
Nous qui au sacrement de la communion
Sommes freres de Christ par divine union,
Avoués fils de Dieu, qui à vostre puissance
A voulu que rendions la deuë obeïssance,
Vous commetant sur nous : & du gouvernement
Faudra que rendiés conte au dernier jugement.
Las ! que de Chrestiens ont enjonché la terre
Entretués pour vous par l'exploit de la guerre !
Que de sang execrable (ô forfaits inhumains !)
Pour rien s'est repandu par fraternelles mains !
. . . .
Chacun de vous renclos aux confins anciens
N'entrepregne plus loin que de garder les siens.
Nul ne passe la borne (ou de la mer barbare,
Ou du fleuve, ou du mont, qui vos païs separe)
Sinon pour s'entraider. La concorde & la Paix
Par vous & vos sugets soit gardee à jamais.

(II, 228-9)

This appeal for peace between Christian countries is not only similar in theme to the following passage from *La Paix* in which Ronsard addresses Henri II,

[55] III, 30-33, 422-68 ; IX, 113, 203 ff.

[56] Baïf's appeal for Christian unity is somewhat ironical if one considers subsequent events, for less than a week after the wedding of Hendri de Navarre and Marguerite de Valois the St Bartholomew massacre took place (August 24th, 1572).

> Bien ? imaginez vous des Flamens la victoire,
> Quel honneur auriez vous d'une si pauvre gloire,
> D'avoir un Roy, Chrestien comme vous, enchainé,
> Et par vostre Paris en triomphe mené ?
> Il vaudroit mieux chasser le Turc hors de la Grece,
> Qui miserable vit soubz le joug de detresse,
> Que prendre un Roy Chrestien, ou de meurtrir de coups
> Un peuple en JESUSCHRIST baptisé comme vous.
>
> (IX, 113-4, 213-20)

but it is also reminiscent of the opening and concluding passages of the
Exhortation pour la Paix of the previous year :

> Non, ne combatez pas, vivez en amitié,
> CHRETIENS, changez vostre ire avecque la pitié,
> Changez à la douceur les rancunes ameres,
> Et ne trampez vos dars dans le sang de vos freres,
> . . . .
> . . . .
> Donc, Paix fille de Dieu, vueille toy souvenir,
> Si je t'invoque à gré, maintenant de venir
> Rompre l'ire des Rois, & pour l'honneur de celle
> Que JESUS CHRIST a faitte au monde universelle
> Entre son Pere & nous, repousse de ta main
> Loing des peuples Chretiens, le Discord inhumain
> Qui les tient acharnez, & vueilles de ta grace
> A jamais nous aymer, & toute notre race.
>
> (IX, 15, 1-4 ; 26, 213-20)

In the same way other lines from Baïf's long final movement point to
recollections from Ronsard's *La Paix*. Baïf's

> O ROIS pensés à vous : & puis que Dieu vous done
> Le beau don de la Paix, chacun de vous s'adone
> A l'aimer & garder.
>
> (II, 228)

is textually very close to Ronsard's

> Donc, Sire, puisque Dieu (qui de vostre couronne,
> Et de vous prent le soing) Paix sa fille vous donne,
> Present qu'il n'avoit fait aux Princes vos ayeux :
> Gardez la tousjours bien :
>
> (IX, 115, 237-40)

whilst the punishments called down by Baïf on the first person to break the
peace,

> . . . . Qui premier l'enfreindra,
> Qu'il tombe à la mercy du Roy qu'il assaudra.
> Que de son ennemy son païs soit la proye :
> Qu'en son trone royal jamais ne se revoye :
> Jamais ceux de son sang n'y puissent revenir,
> Puis que la bonne Paix il n'a sceu maintenir.
>
> (II, 228-9)

is similar in theme at least to this passage of *La Paix* :

> Donne nous que celluy qui sera le moyen
> Entre ces deux grans Roys de rompre ton lien

Meure trahi des siens d'une playe cruelle,
Et qu'aux champs les mâtins luy suçent la cervelle,
Que ses enfans banis puissent mourir de fain,
Sans trouver un amy qui leur jette du pain.

(IX, 116, 263-8)

Finally, a major aspect of Ronsard's *Exhortation pour la Paix* was the appeal for a new crusade against the infidel countries in the name of Christian unity,[57] and this idea reappears in *La Paix* of the following year :

O Paix fille de Dieu, qui nous viens réjouir

. . . .

Chasse, je te supply, la guerre & les querelles
Bien loing du bord Chrestien de sur les Infidelles,
Turcs, Parthes, Mammelus, Scythes & Sarrasins,
Et sur ceux qui du Nil sont les proches voisins.

(IX, 115, 247, 253-6)

Although this is not an uncommon motif of the poetry of the age written in celebration of peace,[58] within the framework of the frequent thematic and textual reminiscences from Ronsard's peace poems Baïf's brief reference to this idea,

DIEU veille detourner la discorde mortelle
D'entre les ROIS Chrestiens sur le peuple infidelle,

(II, 229)

may well have been suggested by Ronsard.

What has been suggested here is that Baïf's *Hymne de la Paix* is not so much a conscious or direct imitation of one or more of Ronsard's four poems on peace as an original and poetic re-expression of assimilated ideas and themes. Everything points to a recent re-reading by Baïf of Ronsard's *Ode de la Paix*, and, more especially, of his *Exhortation pour la Paix*, *La Paix* and *Chant de Liesse* of 1558-59,[59] for the overall plan and development of ideas in Baïf's "hymne", as well as the principal movements, themes and some verbal and stylistic echoes, clearly suggest Ronsard's peace poems as a major inspiration.[60] Baïf's "hymne" is in fact a perfect example of the process of imitation defined by du Bellay in the *Deffence et Illustration* in terms of innutrition.[61]

[57] IX, 17-20, 27-80. Same idea in the *Chant de Liesse*, ll. 121-4.

[58] Same idea in Louis le Roy, *De Pace* (1559), du Bellay, *De pace inter principes christianos inuenda* (*Poemata*, 1558), Belleau, *Chant de la Paix* (in *La Bergerie*, 1572).

[59] There is evidence of the influence of Ronsard's *Exhortation pour la Paix* and *La Paix* elsewhere in Baïf's *Poemes*. Cf. a passage describing the reign of Peace in Baïf's *A Monseigneur de Lansac* (II, 379-80) and Ronsard, IX, 24-5, 183-194 ; 115-6, 257-62. Although some of the details in Ronsard have their source in a paean of Bacchylides preserved in Stobaeus, *Florilegium*, LV (*On Peace*), Baïf's debt is to Ronsard alone.

[60] The actual structure of Baïf's "hymne" bears some resemblance to Ronsard's "hymnes" of 1555-6. Written in alexandrine rhyming couplets with a prologue-dedication and a long central section on a single subject (Peace), Baïf's "hymne" differs notably from the genre as established by Ronsard in that it does not end with an invocation or apostrophe.

[61] Referring to the way in which the Romans enriched their originally impoverished language by assimilating the best works of Greek literature, du Bellay speaks of the Romans " immitant les meilleurs aucteurs Grecz, se transformant en eux, les devorant, & apres les avoir bien digerez, les convertissant en sang & nouriture " (op. cit., Book I, chapter VII).

Something of the same technique of innutrition can be seen in a satirical poem of *Les Passetems* entitled *A Henry Estienne*, the source of which Augé-Chiquet[62] gives as Horace, *Satires*, II, vi. The influence of Horace, however, is limited to the general theme of the contrast between the peace of the countryside and the turbulence of the city and to a single textual echo in the evocation of rustic pleasures.[63] For the satirical description of the noise and hustle and bustle of Paris, Baïf, like Boileau later,[64] owes nothing to Horace but prefers, as will be seen, to contaminate two passages from Juvenal and Martial :

> Donc, Estienne, tu te redonnes
> A ta ville, & tu abandonnes
> Des chams le sejour gracieux ?
> Donc le repos solacieux
> De nos chams plus ne te recree,
> Mais le bruit de Paris t'agree :
> Comme tu as bien merité
> Jouy du bien de ta cité :
> Tousjours à tes oreilles tonne
> Le tonnelier coignant sa tonne.
> Le tailleur s'en vienne tailler
> Sa pierre pour te reveiller
> Le matin : Et qu'au soir t'essourde
> Le son de quelque cloche lourde.
> Le charratier le long du jour
> Criant ne te donne sejour,
> Importun devant ta fenestre :
> Et ce quand plus tu voudrois estre
> En repos pour jouir des dons
> Que des Muses nous pretendons.
> Et si tu vas parmi les rues,
> Sois tant que point ne te remues
> De crieurs de fien empressé.
> Ou le soliciteur pressé
> Donne tel coup en ta poitrine
> Qu'il t'en face ployer l'echine :
> Le portefange tumbereau
> Souille de fange ton manteau.

---

[62] Op. cit., p. 263, note 1.

[63] Cf. Baïf :

> Et pour mieux les heures seduire
> Nous avons coustume de lire,
> Ou les vers qu'Ovide a sonnez,
> Ou ceux qu'Horace a façonnez,
> Ou les raillardes chançonnettes
> Que le Syracusain a faittes,
> Ou du Berger Latin les chants
> Qui monstrent le labour des chams.   (IV, 418-9)

and Horace :

> o rus, quando ego te aspiciam ! quandoque licebit
> nunc veterum libris, nunc somno et inertibus horis,
>   ducere sollicitae iucunda oblivia vitae ! (loc. cit., ll. 60-2)

Apart from this reminiscence, Baïf's account of country pleasures is original.

[64] *Satires*, VI.

Rencontre une charogne morte
Que loin en la voirie on porte :
Trouve quelqu'un de peste atteint
Qui sur la siviere se plaint :
Endure des maux plus de mille
Ordinaires dedans la ville :
Soule toy de tous les ennuis
Qu'on y a les jours & les nuits.

(IV, 417-8)

It is Martial, XII, lvii, lines 3-17, who, in the context of a satirical contrast between city and country life, provides Baïf with the account of noises which interrupt concentration and disturb the peace :

nec cogitandi, Sparse, nec quiescendi
in urbe locus est pauperi. negant vitam
ludi magistri mane, nocte pistores,
aerariorum marculi die toto ;
hinc otiosus sordidam quatit mensam
Neroniana nummularius massa,
illinc palucis malleator Hispanae
tritum nitenti fuste verberat saxum ;
nec turba cessat entheata Bellonae,
nec fasciato naufragus loquax trunco,
a matre doctus nec rogare Iudaeus,
nec sulpuratae lippus institor mercis.
numerare pigri damna qui potest somni,
dicet quot aera verberent manus urbis,
cum secta Colcho Luna vapulat rhombo.

Baïf, it will be noted, takes only the general idea from Martial and, apart from the reference to the beating of a hammer on stone, finds his own illustrations of city noise.

Baïf's debt to Juvenal III is a little more substantial, although again the French poet's original contribution and freedom of adaptation must be emphasised. Apart from the general antithesis between the city and the country, Baïf borrows from Juvenal's satire of Rome the details of the noise of wagon drovers, the crowded streets,[65] the blow in the chest and the splattering of mud :

Plurimus hic aeger moritur vigilando (set ipsum
languorem peperit cibus inperfectus et haerens
ardenti stomacho), nam quae meritoria somnum
admittunt ? magnis opibus dormitur in urbe.
inde caput morbi. raedarum transitus arto
vicorum in flexu et stantis convicia mandrae
eripient somnum Druso vitulisque marinis.
. . . .
. . . . nobis properantibus opstat
unda prior, magno populus premit agmine lumbos
qui sequitur ; ferit hic cubito, ferit assere duro

---

[65] There is a brief reference to the crowded streets in Horace, *Satires*, II, vi, 28 (" luctandum in turba et facienda iniuria tardis "), but Juvenal's influence is much more significant here.

alter, at hic tignum capiti incutit, ille metretam.
pinguia crura luto, planta mox undique magna
calcor, et in digito clavus mihi militis haeret.
(loc. cit., ll. 232-8, 243-8)

In addition there is a reminiscence of Juvenal, III, 32,

. . . . portandum ad busta cadaver,

in Baïf's,

Rencontre une charogne morte
Que loin en la voirie on porte.

★   ★   ★

Besides noting the major sources of certain passages and poems included for the first time in Baïf's *Euvres en rime*, we have seen in passing how Baïf's art of poetic composition and adaptation of source material cover a variety of techniques. *A Monsieur de Mauru* reveals a rather slavish paraphrase of a single text (Menander), which gives little scope for personal interpretation and which bears out what certain critics have written about Baïf's extensive humanist knowledge being a limitation to original expression and an aspect of his lack of poetic imagination.[66] The *Vie des Chams* owes a debt to multiple sources, and principally to texts of Pliny, Menander and Virgil, contaminated with greater flexibility and arranged in sequence so as to form a coherent and poetic unity. Finally, we have noted two successful examples of a process of innutrition, as defined in the *Deffence et Illustration*, in which Baïf gives original expression to a general development of ideas and themes assimilated from several texts. This process may either take the form of an assimilation of a number of texts from a single author (Ronsard, with distant echoes of Tibullus, in the *Hymne de la Paix*) or from several different sources centred on a common theme (Horace, Juvenal and Martial in *A Henry Estienne*).

MALCOLM QUAINTON

Lancaster

---

[66] Cf. Augé-Chiquet, op. cit., pp. 583-4 ; Chamard, *Histoire de la Pléiade*, III, 201 ; IV, 44 (where Chamard talks of Baïf's work in these terms : " la traduction y tient une place excessive, ce qui dénote . . . pauvreté d'imagination, manque d'idées originales ".)

V

THE TRAGEDIES OF JACQUES DE LA TAILLE[1]

Jacques de la Taille's two tragedies have attracted little attention from scholars and literary historians, and *Daïre* and *La Mort d'Alexandre* have not been reprinted in modern times. A handful of his lyrics are found in anthologies, and Pierre Han has made a study of his treatise on quantitative versification, *La Maniere de faire des vers en français, comme en grec et en latin*.[2] Faguet, Rigal, Raymond Lebègue and Elliott Forsyth all mention Jacques de la Taille's plays in passing, but these have not been the object of detailed examination since the late nineteenth century when G. Baguenault de Puchesse brought out his useful article " Jean et Jacques de la Taille : étude biographique et littéraire ".[3] Neither René de Maulde who edited Jean de la Taille's works, nor T. A. Daley who wrote a biographical study of him, pays much heed to his younger brother.[4] This neglect of Jacques de la Taille is understandable, especially since even his contemporaries appear not to have considered him important. He could hardly claim attention while so much research remained to be done on the major French dramatists of the sixteenth century. Modern critics have, moreover, invariably come to Jacques de la Taille via his brother Jean, and this has resulted in his being somewhat overshadowed. Yet with the deeper understanding of the specific qualities of French Renaissance tragedy which has come in the last decades, it is now possible to see that Jacques de la Taille's plays have real merits.

In 1572 the first of Jacques de la Taille's works was published, a small collection of occasional pieces, *Le Recueil des inscriptions, anagrammatismes et autres œuvres*. It is printed on the final pages of the volume containing *Saül le furieux* and a number of his brother's poems. *Le Recueil* is prefaced by an epistle to the reader by Jean de la Taille, and this is the main source

---

[1] This article is based on my unpublished Ph.D. dissertation, " The Tragedies of Jean and Jacques de la Taille " (Cambridge University Library, 1969).

Quotations from *Le Recueil des inscriptions, anagrammatismes et autres œuvres poétiques* of 1572 are from the British Museum copy of Jean de la Taille's *Saül le furieux* etc., shelf-mark 1073.d.4(2). Those from Jacques de la Taille's other three works, *Daïre*, *La Mort d'Alexandre*, and *La Maniere de faire des vers en français, comme en grec et en latin*—all of 1573—are taken from the copies kept at the Bodleian Library, Oxford.

[2] Pierre Han, " Jacques de la Taille's *La Maniere* : A Critical Edition " (Columbia University, New York, 1960—Mic 61-860). Dr Han presents a brief summary of his dissertation in " Un essai abortif de la Renaissance ", *Romance Notes* V (1963-64), 72-5.

[3] E. Faguet, *La Tragédie française au XVIe siècle*, second ed. (Paris, 1912), pp. 185-86 ; E. Rigal, " Le Théâtre de la Renaissance ", *Histoire de la langue et littérature française*, ed. Petit de Julleville, III, 6 ; Raymond Lebègue, *La Tragédie française de la Renaissance*, second ed. (Bruxelles, 1954), p. 38 ; Elliott Forsyth, *La Tragédie française de Jodelle à Corneille* (Paris, 1962), p. 150 ; G. Baguenault de Puchesse, " Jean et Jacques de la Taille : étude biographique et littéraire sur deux poètes du XVIe siècle ", *Lectures et Mémoires de l'Académie de Sainte-Croix* VI (1889).

[4] Jean de la Taille, *Œuvres*, ed. René de Maulde, 4 vols., (Paris, 1878-82) ; Tatham Ambersley Daley, *Jean de la Taille, 1533-1608* ; *étude historique et littéraire* (Paris, 1934).

of biographical information about Jacques. (Both La Croix du Maine and Du Verdier mention him, but their notes offer nothing additional. The entry about Jacques de la Taille in Guillaume Colletet's *Vies des poètes français*, which survives in Aimé Martin's nineteenth-century transcript [Bibliothèque Nationale, Nouv. Acq. fr. 3073, Ff. 284-5], is valueless.) Jacques de la Taille was born in 1542 at the family home at Bondaroy in Gastinois ; he was around seven years younger than his brother Jean. His father belonged to the minor nobility and adhered to the reformed religion, though he does not seem to have handed on to his children a fanatical faith. No doubt after some elementary education at home, Jacques de la Taille, like his brother before him, was sent to Paris for further studies. Jean de la Taille would have us believe that his father was motivated solely by a disinterested love of culture and had no intention of making his sons " gens d'Eglise, ou de Justice ". The family's religious beliefs ruled out the possibility of a career in the Church. On the other hand, it can hardly be insignificant that after six years in Paris Jean de la Taille went to Orleans to read Civil Law. Whatever their father's intentions, the humanist training which the brothers La Taille received served, as it did for many writers of this period, as a preliminary to original composition in French.[5] Not much is known about Jacques de la Taille's years in Paris. He studied under a preceptor in a private house together with a number of other youths, including eventually a younger brother and a cousin. This was a common arrangement which enabled the children of Protestant families to profit from some of the teaching given in the Paris colleges without their running the risk of persecution. For example, it is recorded that until Easter 1562 the young Philippe Duplessis-Mornay was able to stay " à Paris chez M. Prebet, qui logeoit derrière le college de Boncourt, et frequentoit lors les leçons de la seconde class avec apparent progrez, et sans participer à l'idolastrie. Plusieurs enfans d'honneste maison estoient nourris ensemble, entr'-aultres les plus jeunes de Rambouillet et ceux de Bellenave."[6] It would appear that Jacques de la Taille was a boarder in a house like this, and thus he was able to attend lectures by Jean Daurat and become aware of the latest developments in the arts. Before long, Jean de la Taille returned to Paris to join his brother. He had not found the study of law to his taste. Instead, he was full of enthusiasm for Ronsard and Du Bellay " qui commençoient lors à voler par la bouche des hommes ". Jacques had, if we are to believe his brother, already become a remarkable classical scholar, and Jean now taught him " tout ce que je sçavoys de l'Art Poètique ". Jacques de la Taille wrote his first plays when he was only sixteen. But he was not to live much longer, and in April 1562, at the age of just twenty, he was the victim of some virulent infectious disease.

[5] Cf. Gilbert Gadoffre's discussion of the training of Ronsard and other Pléiade poets in *Ronsard par lui-même* (Paris, 1964), pp. 10-14.

[6] *Mémoires de Charlotte Arbaleste sur la vie de Duplessis-Mornay son mari*, in *Mémoires et correspondance de Duplessis-Mornay* (Paris, 1824), pp. 18-19.

Before his premature death, Jacques de la Taille had written several works. Some of these were never printed and have been lost; among them were four tragedies (*Athamant*, *Progné*, *Niobé* and a play about Dido), one or more comedies, and some poems intended to demonstrate the principles put forward in *La Maniere de faire des vers*. This treatise and the two tragedies, *Daïre* and *La Mort d'Alexandre*, appeared in separate volumes printed at Paris by Fédéric Morel only in 1573, eleven years after their author's death. Jean de la Taille had made a selection from among the papers left by his brother of the works which seemed to him " de meilleure veuë pour soustenir la lumiere ". He had, moreover, " servy (en y mettant la derniere main) de Curateur, ou de Parrain, comme à pauvres orphelins, ou posthumes, comme disent les Legistes ". (Vauquelin de la Fresnaye refers in his *Art poétique* in similar terms to Sainte-Marthe's revision of La Péruse's *Médée*.) That some of Jacques de la Taille's tragedies have not survived is probably of little consequence, but the fact that his plays were published only belatedly reduced their chances of making much impact on his contemporaries. There is, indeed, nothing to substantiate the boast made by Jacques in a prefatory note to *La Maniere de faire des vers*, that his work had already won the praise of the great ladies and nobles of the court. Like his brother, he apparently stood aloof from the habit of writers at this time of exchanging laudatory liminary poems. The importance of the one exception to this generalization is reduced by abnormal circumstances. Anxious perhaps to signal his return from Rome, Du Bellay wrote a sonnet praising Jacques de la Taille ; around the same time he composed a piece in a similar vein for Jacques Grévin.[7] After Du Bellay's death Jacques de la Taille returned the compliment in a pair of sonnets intended for his *Tombeau*. But neither Du Bellay's sonnet (which is not signed, but whose author is indicated by the motto *Caelo Musa beat*) nor Jacques de la Taille's two poems were printed until 1573 when they all appeared at the end of the volume containing *La Mort d'Alexandre*. By this late date, the relationship with Du Bellay, which is hardly likely to have been close, had lost whatever publicity value it might have had.

The possible influence of Jacques de la Taille's work on the tragedies of Robert Garnier, Alexandre Hardy, and Sir William Alexander, Earl of Stirling, has already been investigated, though with only meagre rewards.[8] Jacques de la Taille's own very considerable debts to earlier writers have, on the other hand, been ignored. It is revealing to study how he adapts historical material for dramatic purpose, and even more interesting to note

[7] See Raymond Lebègue, " Dans l'entourage de Du Bellay ", *Bibliothèque d'Humanisme et Renaissance* IV (1944), 171-6, and Henri Chamard, *Du Bellay* (Lille, 1900), p. 476.

[8] See Marie-Madeleine Mouflard, *Robert Garnier*, III, *Les Sources* (La Roche-sur-Yon, 1964), pp. 259-67 ; E. Rigal, *Alexandre Hardy et le théâtre français* (Paris, 1889), pp. 358-84 ; and the introduction by L. E. Kastner and H. B. Charlton to *The Poetical Works of Sir William Alexander, Earl of Stirling*, Scottish Text Society, N.S. 11, Vol. I (Edinburgh, 1921).

that he takes a contemporary literary work as the model for *La Mort d'Alexandre*. The important part played in original composition in the Renaissance by the imitation of other literary works has come to be more clearly appreciated in recent times.[9] Nineteenth-century source-hunters were somtimes horrified by what they found. But in the Renaissance there was nothing disreputable about taking from the classics (or from an eminent contemporary) details, lengthy passages, or even basic structural patterns, and using them in one's own poems. What the poet was required to do was to recast and incorporate convincingly whatever he had selected for imitation. In *De l'institution des enfants* Montaigne is scathing about French authors who copy the classics incompetently, but his concern is not with the impropriety of imitation, but with the foolishness of failing to integrate what has been imitated. A plagiarist is a sneak-thief, but there is nothing furtive about literary imitation in the Renaissance, and indeed the savour of many of the borrowings comes out fully only when we are aware of the source and able to recognise a deft and apt reworking of second-hand material.

The main historical source of *Daïre* and *La Mort d'Alexandre* is a fairly obvious one, *The History of Alexander the Great* by Quintus Curtius. The popularity of this book in France in the sixteenth century is shown by the number of translations published, though there is no clear evidence that La Taille used a French version of the text. Quintus Curtius is little respected nowadays, but the criticisms made by W. W. Tarn, for example, serve paradoxically to pin-point features of this historian's work likely to appeal to Renaissance sensibilities which admired Seneca so whole-heartedly.[10] He creates a colourful and lively impression of the heroes of the past, though he is little concerned with historical accuracy. A major feature is his inclusion of grand speeches supposedly delivered by the various characters involved. As Tarn puts it, " he is steeped in rhetorical training and writes like a rhetorician." That Jacques de la Taille was impressed by the orations inserted in *The History of Alexander the Great* is shown by the fact that he is sometimes content to reproduce them in verse-translation. An example may be taken from Act II, Scene 2, of *Daïre*, in which the Persian king appeals to his troops for loyal support :

> " Si cum ingnavis ", inquit, " et pluris qualemcumque vitam quam honestam mortem aestimantibus Fortuna me iunxisset, tacerem potius quam frustra verba consumerem. Sed maiore quam vellem documento et virtutem vestram et fidem expertus, magis etiam coniti debeo ut dignus talibus amicis sim, quam dubitari an vestri similes, adhuc sitis ". (*Historia*, V. 8. 6 and 7)

[9] See G. Castor, *Pléiade Poetics* (Cambridge, 1964), pp. 63-76, and John Sparrow, " Latin verse of the High Renaissance ", in *Italian Renaissance Studies*, ed. E. F. Jacob (London, 1960), pp. 354-409.

[10] W. W. Tarn, *Alexander the Great*, 2 vols. (Cambridge, 1948), see especially Vol. II, pp. 91-92. In addition to consulting various sixteenth-century editions, I have used the edition of Quintus Curtius's *History of Alexander the Great* in the Loeb Classical Library, edited and translated by J. C. Rolfe.

Si DIEU m'avoit (ô Princes et Soudards)
Donné des gens ou traistres ou couards,
Je me tairois pour ne parler en vain,
Mais ayant fait l'essay trop plus certain
Que je ne veux, tant de la bienveillance
Dont vous m'aymez, que de vostre vaillance,
Je ne serois digne de vous avoir,
Si par parolle aumoins je ne fais voir,
Que vos bienfaicts je ne vas oubliant. (*Daïre*, F12^v)

Jacques de la Taille does not always follow the wording of Quintus Curtius
so closely as this, but the influence of the Latin text is apparent everywhere
in the two tragedies in the phrasing of the speeches as well as in the various
incidents. A final feature bound to attract Jacques de la Taille and his
contemporaries was Quintus Curtius's general outlook. For Quintus Curtius,
history is a record of the workings of Fortune, an inexorable force which
even the greatest men cannot withstand, though they may endure it with
stoic fortitude.

From Quintus Curtius Jacques de la Taille took virtually all the incidents
found in *Daïre*. For additional detail, he turned to Amyot's translation of
Plutarch's *Vies des hommes illustres*.[11] This appeared first in 1558, so Jacques
de la Taille would be among the very earliest of the many Renaissance playwrights to make use of this source. Everything taken from Plutarch is
carefully integrated with the outline found in Quintus Curtius. Jacques de
la Taille invents Daïre's opening monologue in which he bewails his mis-
fortunes, and adds a certain life to the first act by introducing the trusty
Prince Artabaze who is able to persuade the king that an appeal to the
troops may be effective. In the next three acts, Daïre is shown as the victim
of a plot mounted against him by his satraps as Alexandre's army draws
ever closer. Quintus Curtius is the source of most of the incidents, though
some of the material has to be put into dramatic form. Daïre is taken captive
by the conspirators and eventually dies of wounds, but Alexandre's army
arrives to defeat the Persians and put the conspirators to flight. Some
semblance of dramatic movement is given by La Taille's treatment of the
conspiracy and by his presentation of Daïre who oscillates between impotent
despair and manly resolution. But the play is dominated by the personality
of Alexandre, whose approach is the decisive factor in the opening scenes
and who appears in Act V to listen with pity and indignation to the account
of Daïre's ignominious death. (His role is, in fact, very similar to that of
David in Jean de la Taille's *Saül le furieux*.)

Quintus Curtius provided only the barest outline of an account of the
last days of Alexander the Great, and Plutarch, though the source of interesting detail, was not much help to Jacques de la Taille in shaping the plot
of *La Mort d'Alexandre*. Convention required that the plots of tragedies

---

[11] I have used the Bibliothèque de la Pléiade edition, with notes by Gérard Walter,
of Amyot's translation of Plutarch's *Vies des hommes illustres*.

should have a historical foundation. (This may account for Jean de la Taille's refusal to have his brother's *Athamant* printed : in *De l'art de la tragédie* he insists that in *Saül le furieux* " je n'ay des histoires fabuleuses mendié les fureurs d'un Athamant, d'un Hercules, ny d'un Roland. . .").[12] Like *Daïre*, *La Mort d'Alexandre* is based on the works of two well-known historians, but La Taille disregards the reservations which both express regarding the veracity of the tale that Alexander was poisoned. He also is not at all inhibited in re-organising his material for greater dramatic impact.

As regards incident and style, *La Mort d'Alexandre* owes in fact a great deal to a literary model. Raymond Lebègue has drawn attention to the importance of the Neo-Latin poets, principally George Buchanan and Marc-Antoine Muret, as mentors and exemplars to authors, especially dramatists, writing in French in the mid-sixteenth century.[13] Jean de la Taille who was proud to recall that he had heard Muret's lectures may be counted among them. It is therefore interesting to find in *La Mort d'Alexandre* many unmistakable signs of the influence of Muret's Latin tragedy, *Julius Caesar*. Another reworking of Muret's play, Jacques Grévin's *César*, was first performed and published in 1561 ; there is, however, no indication that either dramatist knew of the other's work, though both were in Paris at this time and might easily have come into contact. In her very recent edition of Grévin's *César*, Dr Ginsberg, working quite independently, has reached conclusions the same as my own.[14] Muret's *Julius Caesar* (first printed in his *Juvenilia* of 1553) must have already been well-known, and it is a safe assumption that the young writers associated with the Collège de Boncourt were all familiar with it. Just like Ronsard, Muret was becoming a classic in his own life-time, which meant that it was as legitimate to take his works as a literary model as to turn to Quintus Curtius for historical information. The fact that Plutarch wrote his lives of Alexander and Caesar in parallel adds to the appropriateness of the literary model taken by Jacques de la Taille. From Muret, Jacques de la Taille does not take incidents so much as suggestions about the possible dramatic treatment of a number of incidents found in Quintus Curtius and Plutarch. The plot of *La Mort d'Alexandre* is, in fact, simpler than that of *Daïre*. In Act I Alexandre arrives at Babylon, self-confident and ready for further conquests. He disregards a soothsayer's warning, and fails to realise that his life is being threatened by a conspiracy. Act IV and the first part of Act V are devoted to a death-bed scene, as the

[12] See G. Giovanni's two articles, " The Connection between Tragedy and History in Ancient Criticism ", *Philological Quarterly* XXII (1943), 308-14, and " Historical Realism and the Tragic Emotions in Renaissance Criticism ", *Philological Quarterly* XXXII (1953), 304-20. In " L'Influence des romanciers sur les dramaturges français de la fin du XVIe siècle ", *Bibliothèque d'Humanisme et Renaissance* XVII (1965), 74-9, Raymond Lebègue states that it was only about 1575 that the romances began to be used as sources of plots for tragedies.

[13] Raymond Lebègue, " L'Influence du théâtre néo-latin sur le théâtre sérieux en langue française ", *Humanisme et Renaissance* VI (1939), 41-47.

[14] Jacques Grévin, *César*, ed. Ellen S. Ginsberg, Textes Littéraires français no. 179 (Geneva : Droz, 1971), pp. 38-40.

poisoned hero gradually comes to terms with his fate and takes farewell of his friends. Once again a conspiracy has given an impression of dramatic movement, but after the report that Alexandre has been poisoned, the action lags (as it tends to do in other plays derived from Muret's *Julius Caesar*), though Jacques de la Taille, like Grévin, avoids the apotheosis of the hero which rather unsatisfactorily concludes his Latin model. Instead, we hear first Alexandre's death-bed speech and then a lament over him by Sigambre and her daughter-in-law, Saptine, Daïre's widow, who had been treated well ever since her husband's death and sees the Macedonian king as the embodiment of all human virtue.

If one reads Jacques de la Taille's historical sources and compares them with his finished plays it becomes clear that he has invented remarkably little. But he has carried out quite a large-scale re-organisation of his material, taking, in the case of *La Mort d'Alexandre*, several ideas from Muret's *Julius Caesar*, both as regards form and expression. He imposes unity of time, using it to build up tension as the conspirators in both plays resolve that they must take action this very day. The *in medias res* convention provides ample opportunity for grand speeches recalling what has happened before, just as the prohibition of violence on stage offers scope for graphic messenger-speeches. As in Jean de la Taille's tragedies, unity of place is rather widely interpreted. The action of each of the tragedies is confined to a single city, and there is nothing of the freedom found in the irregular plays or in English drama. But in neither play does the action take place on a single set ; instead, some means—perhaps nothing more than an opening in the back-wall of the stage covered by a curtain—is required to enable the fourth act to take place within the hero's tent, whereas the rest of the play may be supposed to take place in front of it. Jacques de la Taille satisfactorily characterises the chorus in the two plays as a troop of soldiers who comment on the action and even help to some extent with the exposition ; the chorus is used in the conventional way to separate the acts of the tragedy, but it is interesting to note that Jacques de la Taille, for once differing from his brother on a point of dramatic practice, also has short concluding choruses after Act V. In all other respects, Jacques de la Taille's dramatic technique is perfectly conventional, and it is only in his handling of the rule of three interlocutors in Act III of *Alexandre* that he appears to have some difficulty. Otherwise, he displays genuine competence in his treatment of a complex art-form. Much of what he does with his material cannot fail to seem quite obvious to readers used to the French classics. But in the early 1560's Jacques de la Taille's skill in shaping his historical material is an indication of real ability.

For Jacques de la Taille, as for his contemporaries, tragedy is the presentation in due form of a notable calamity. Much effort is taken to impress on us the magnitude and inevitability of the disaster, but the moral significance of the tragic event is hardly investigated. Attention is concentrated on the way the hero, to his companions' admiration, comes to the realisation that the only resource available to him is to accept whatever Fortune has in store. The death of Alexander the Great—" le plus grand homme simplement homme ", as Montaigne, a man of Jacques de la Taille's generation, was to call him—could hardly be bettered as an example of astonishing prosperity cut brutally short in the hour of triumph. From Plutarch emerges too the picture of a stoic sage, sober and chaste in life, noble in death. Quintus Curtius provides ample justification for presenting Daïre too as " la fable et le jouet de Fortune ". She may smile sometimes, but once a man has reached the top of her wheel, Fortune capriciously delights to dash him down. In his treatment of this material which fully satisfies convention, Jacques de la Taille follows procedures which resemble those adopted by his brother, especially in *Saül le furieux*. The dedicatory epistles provided for *Daïre* and *La Mort d'Alexandre* by Jean de la Taille stress their relevance to present-day troubles. It is not a question of an allegory of contemporary politics or anything of that sort. The aim, rather, is to offer a portrayal of the way Fortune attacked even the greatest heroes of antiquity and of the manner in which they overcame calamity with fortitude. Such examples should serve as both consolations and lessons when modern men find themselves in difficulties. An extra dimension is added by the fact that in both plays the downfall of the hero is connected with, if not exactly caused by, disloyalty. This makes the tragedies all the more relevant to France in the second half of the sixteenth century, and it is interesting to note that in both of Jean de la Taille's tragedies too the plot is complicated by divisions within the state.

Yet dissension is, in *La Mort d'Alexandre*, only the immediate cause of the downfall of the Macedonian king, whilst the satraps' conspiracy in *Daïre* is just the final episode in the destruction of the Persian king whose military defeat is itself presented as outstanding proof of Fortune's fickleness. The conspirators talk of overweening pride and so on, but the heroes do not consider that they are being punished for any wrong-doing on their part. Instead, they protest that they are demonstrations of Fortune's spitefulness towards those she has perhaps favoured too much. Even more weight is given to this interpretation of the tragic event by the chorus and by the final speeches. Just as in *Saül le furieux*, the final act of *Daïre* is devoted to the portrayal of the antagonist's sorrow at his adversary's misfortune and of his admiration for his personal qualities. Like David, Alexandre does not exult in his victory and tends, indeed, even to overlook the fact that he has served as Fortune's tool, while the conspirators, like the Amalekite Soldier, are roundly condemned for disloyalty and wickedness. Similarly, at the end of *La Mort d'Alexandre* the conspirators again take to their heels, while Sigambre and Saptine launch into a threnody for the dead king, recalling only his many virtues. In *De l'art de la tragédie*, Jean de la Taille writes that tragic heroes should be neither " Seigneurs extremement meschants " nor " gents de bien et de saincte vie ". Jacques too seems to have been aware of this concept. Yet in *Daïre* and *La Mort d'Alexandre* there emerges no sense of a genuine causal connection between misdeeds and their due, if disproportionately harsh, punishment. The heroes' wrongs are no more seen as the cause of their downfall than as a justification for their subjects' disloyalty.

All the same, the conspiracies in the two tragedies serve a distinct dramatic function. One of Jean de la Taille's most important observations about writing tragedies concerns the plot ; in *De l'art de la tragédie* he writes that " c'est le principal point d'une Tragedie de la sçavoir bien disposer, bien bastir, et la deduire de sorte qu'elle change, transforme, manie, et tourne l'esprit des escoutans deçà delà et faire qu'ils voyent maintenant une joye tournee tout soudain en tristesse, et maintenant au rebours, à l'exemple des choses humaines ". Yet the basic conception of the tragic event shared by the brothers La Taille with other French playwrights of the period would seem to be hardly compatible with this stipulation. The problem was to find some means of giving a semblance of dramatic movement to plots while adhering to the principle that events are determined, not by men, but by Fortune or God. In *Saül le furieux*, Jean de la Taille's solution was to compose a plot portraying the Israelite king's various attempts to find out what must befall him ; he is first struck down with madness, but recovers sufficiently to journey to Endor to consult with the Witch and finally returns to the battle-field where he discusses his plight with his squire before rushing off to his death in battle. A fair number of events happen in *Saül le furieux*, but the king does nothing which either causes or in any way alters the eventual calamity. Very similar points can be made about the conspiracies in *Daïre* and *La Mort d'Alexandre* ; these are not plays about the subversion of the throne of Daïre by his satraps or about poisoning of Alexandre by traitors, but lively portrayals of the destruction of these two great human beings by Fortune. The conspirators' discussions, like the more trusty comrades' speeches expressing loyalty, serve to cast more light on the heroes' characters, providing a relief from monologues and discussions with sympathisers. Exposition becomes less of a formality when a plot is being hatched. Most important of all, as the conspirators make plans, attempt to carry them through, find their schemes momentarily checked, so that a delusive hope is born in the hero, and eventually achieve their immediate objectives, a variety of moods and a semblance of dramatic movement are produced.

For French sixteenth-century audiences and readers, tragedies were, however, interesting quite as much for their rhetorical qualities as for their dramatic liveliness. It was primarily because of the opportunities they offered for stylistic elaboration that Du Bellay commended the writing of tragedies in *La Deffence et illustration*. In *Daïre* and *La Mort d'Alexandre* no effort is spared to make the language eloquent and expressive, especially

in the long speeches devoted either to accounts of past events and of off-
stage action or to presentations of the hero's mood. La Taille shows less
interest in scenes devoted to argument and debate and, like his brother, he
makes little use of stichomythia, perhaps because of his limited ability at
coining *sentences*, those single-line formulations of a general moral truth that
are a feature of the style of other sixteenth-century playwrights. In *La
Mort d'Alexandre* La Taille uses the alexandrine throughout, except, of
course, for the choruses which are in lyric metres, whereas in the dialogues
of *Daïre* decasyllables and alexandrines are both employed. It would probably be mistaken to ascribe much importance to this change. In the early
1560s there was general agreement that heroic metres should be employed
in tragedies, and this naturally meant that the octosyllabic line, for example,
should not be used in them. But the decasyllable and the alexandrine had
equally valid claims to be considered as heroic metres, so the use of both
in *Daïre* could appear perfectly legitimate. Rather than credit Jacques de
la Taille with remarkable foresight about the development of French opinion
as to which metre was alone suitable for tragedy, we may assume there was
something about the use of the alexandrine for a play about Alexander
which appealed to Jacques de la Taille's sense of the fitness of things.

Though a devotee of *La Deffence et illustration*, La Taille is, like his
brother, sober in his use of the various stylistic innovations recommended
by Du Bellay, and he wisely does not go in for the various mutilations of
French words which he considers a writer of quantitative verse might permit
himself. On the other hand, he indulges to the full that passion for peri-
phrasis and learned allusion which can reduce some early Pléiade poetry to
an erudite crossword puzzle. For ornament, La Taille relies on a small stock
of devices which he uses regularly. Among his favourites is the extended
simile ; thus, when lamenting his powerlessness to protect his mother and
his wife, Daïre remarks :

> Hà pauvre que je suis,
> Je ressemble à l'oiseau, qui ses petits nourrit,
> Et qui voit un serpent qui goulu les meurtrit,
> Il n'en oze approcher, toutesfois pour l'amour
> Qu'il porte à sa couvee, il volette alentour
> De son nid malheureux, et s'esbranchant aupres
> De son ennemy sourd, gasouille ses regrets.
>
> (*Daïre*, F5^r)

In the two tragedies there are also quite lengthy passages which aim to
impress by piling up quantities of exotic proper names : thus the syco-
phantic courtier Cleon recalls some of Alexandre's conquests as follows :

> Je tais icy comment vous conquistes la ville
> Qui allaicta Bacchus : je tais comme Taxille,
> L'Emperiere Cleofe, Abiazare, Pore,
> Le paisible Fegel, Portican, et encore
> Mille Rois Indiens, ont experimenté
> Vostre vaillance, Sire, avec vostre bonté.
>
> (*Alexandre*, F7^r)

It is hardly surprising that in *La Maniere de faire des vers* Jacques de la Taille devoted a section to expanding Du Bellay's suggestions about giving appropriate French forms to proper names.

In his tragedies Jacques de la Taille sometimes seems to be straining too hard for effect, and his efforts to be expressive lead to certain excesses for which he has been condemned and even ridiculed. Yet when rhetoricians defined the *style grave*, the only one of the three categories of style suitable for tragedy, they commonly spoke of the employment of " vehement figures ", which may be interpreted to mean wide departures from every-day prose usage. Seen in this context, La Taille's excesses, if still not admirable, are at least understandable. For example, when Alexandre has just entered Babylon, the treacherous Thessalle bursts out :

Va, va, ô fier Tyran, ta fiere tyrannie
Sera par des gents fiers bien fierement punie.

(*Alexandre*, F13ᵛ)

Similarly, when at the very end of his report to Alexandre of Daïre's death, Polystrate quotes the dying king's last words, Jacques de la Taille uses a device which has provoked some hilarity :

O Alexandre adieu quelque part où tu sois,
Ma mere et mes enfans aye en recommenda—
Il ne peust achever, car la mort l'engarda.

(*Daïre*, F35ʳ)

A similar couplet has been discovered in *Orlando furioso*,[15] but perhaps this is not an imitation of Ariosto, but just an extreme form of *aposiopesis*. For the most part, Jacques de la Taille's style, in fact, is simple and straightforward, by comparison with what is found in some French sixteenth-century tragedies ; where he does go too far, this can be accounted for by reference to conventional Renaissance requirements about the " vehement figures " proper in tragic style.

Nothing that may be said in their favour in 1971 can, of course, give Jacques de la Taille's two tragedies any very great prestige. The eleven-year delay before they were offered to the only public likely to become enthusiastic about them destroyed Jacques de la Taille's chance of making a name for himself. Du Bellay compared Jacques de la Taille with Sophocles, and the hyperbolic compliment has predictably failed to withstand the test of time. Yet despite some stylistic excesses the author of *Daïre* and *La Mort d'Alexandre* deserves his place alongside La Péruse, Grévin, Bounin and even Jodelle. In his teens he mastered a complex genre and observed its difficult conventions with a considerable measure of success. Like his brother Jean, Jacques de la Taille also realised that there was a means of creating lively movement in the plot without abandoning the concept of tragedy as a portrayal of the hero's destruction by forces which he is unable to explain or control, but which he gradually comes to accept.

C. N. Smith

University of East Anglia

[15] Reinhold Köhler, " Eine Stelle in Ariostos *Orlando furioso* und Nachahmungen derselben ", *Archiv für Literaturgeschichte* V (1876), 1-5.

VI

A RARE EDITION OF AMYOT'S PLUTARCH

The popularity of Jacques Amyot's translations of Plutarch is indicated by the numerous contemporary editions and contrefaçons.[1] The publication of one such pirate edition of the *Vies des Hommes Illustres* (the first edition of which was produced in Paris in 1559 by Michel Vascosan) was mentioned as early as the second edition (1565), but no copy had come to light until very recently.

The royal privilege accorded to Vascosan in 1560 is confirmed in 1563 and appears in the second edition. In the course of this we read that Amyot has started to reprint his book, " auecques plusieurs grādes corrections et annotatiōs, que nostredit Conseiller a de son labeur inuentees, et aussi par le iugement de plusieurs hommes doctes ". The privilege goes on to say that Amyot " a esté aduerty que vn imprimeur estranger demourant à Anvers a fait, sans son sceu, ne permission de nous, r'imprimer la dicte version en deux formes ". In 1908, René Sturel noted this and commented, " Je n'ai pu trouver aucune de ces deux éditions ni dans les bibliothèques de Paris ni à Anvers (Bibliothèque de la Ville et Musée Plantin). Peut-être ne faudrait-il voir dans cette assertion qu'un prétexte de l'imprimeur pour obtenir une confirmation de son privilège ". Sturel refers also to a later contrefaçon mentioned by Nicéron which was supposed to have appeared in Geneva, chez François Perrin, in 1565, but said that he had not been able to find a copy of it ; he had, however, seen a similar 1567 edition in the Bibliothèque de la Ville at Lyons.[2] In an article in *Modern Language Notes* in 1946[3] Bernard Weinberg discussed two copies which were entirely different and yet both purported to be the first edition. He found the Library of Congress copy (PQ 1601, A6 1559) to be the authentic one. He thought at first that the Princeton copy was the Antwerp contrefaçon, but concluded that it was a copy of Le Preux's 1574 edition, with a false title-page and *achevé d'imprimer* taken from a 1575 work.

Since 1946, however, the book has been rediscovered. There is in the Bibliothèque Nationale a copy of volume two only of this 1564 edition (there should be three volumes in all). Aulotte, in his *Amyot et Plutarque*, has a footnote about this book : " Il est assez naturel qu'une contrefaçon ait été donnée à Anvers, ville de culture française. Nous n'avons cependant retrouvé qu'une contrefaçon anversoise des *Vies* antérieure à 1565, celle de G. Silvius, 1564, entrée récemment à la Bibl. Nat. (16° J.199, t. II seule-

---

[1] Cf. Robert Aulotte, *Amyot et Plutarque, La tradition des Moralia au XVIe siècle, Travaux d'Humanisme et Renaissance* LXIX, Droz, Geneva, 1965.

[2] René Sturel, *Jacques Amyot, traducteur des vies parallèles de Plutarque*, Paris, 1908, p. 109.

[3] Bernard Weinberg, " A false first edition of Amyot's Plutarch ", in *Modern Language Notes* LXI (1946), 454-458.

ment)."[4]. This is all Aulotte has to say about it. It seems that the library has lost the record of where it came from and how it was acquired. On the front of the cover we read in gold lettering the initials " G.L.B" and then underneath, " A.S. 1566 ". I have been unable to decipher these initials.

I have in my possession volume one of the same edition. So far I have not found reference anywhere to any other copy.[5]

The book was published by Guillaume Silvius, "imprimeur du Roy ". Nothing much is known about the early life of this man. Colin Clair writes, " Of his life previous to his arrival in Antwerp, probably towards the end of 1559, there is no record. That he was a native of 's Hertogenbosch we may deduce from the fact that he signed himself ' Gulielmus Silvius Busciducensis ' but the date of his birth is unknown ".[6] We do not know whether he printed anything before 1560. Clair shows that Silvius and Christopher Plantin " at the outset of their careers were in close, if jealous relationship " and that through their joint productions they became a little friendlier.[7] It is interesting to note the different books which Silvius produced around the same time as the edition of Plutarch. The first one we know about is his *Io. Lœgii Rupellani de poeticorum studiorum utilitate* of 1560.[8] In 1563 he translated and published at his own press *Princelijcke devijsen ofte wapenen* by Claude Paradijn and others.[9] In the same year he shows his incipient interest in Plutarch by his publication of *Plutarchi Chœronensis, de liberis educandis Liber a Franc. Fabricio Marcodurano latinus factus, et scholiis illustratus. Additus est Liber Grœce, e manuscriptis exemplaribus, eiusdem Fabricii opera emendatus* ".[10] In 1564, the year of the edition of Plutarch which we are considering, he brought out Dr John Dee's *Monas Hieroglyphica* and *Eenen gheestelycken A.B.C. ghetoghen mit den Psalmen van David* which was later placed on the index.[11] In 1567 there is yet another book concerned with Plutarch, *Le tresor des vies de Plutarque, contenant les beaux dicts et faicts des empereurs, roys, ambassadeurs . . . avec quelques vers singuliers, chansons, oracles et epitaphes . . . en l'honneur d'iceux* ". The prefatory letter to the "Noble Seigneur, M. Franchois de Hellefault, Abbé de Sainct Pierre " says that it was destined " à l'usage de ceux qui n'ont grand moien d'acheter l'œuure entiere des Vies des Hommes Illustres, tant Grecz que Romains, comparees tres doctement les vnes avec les autres ".[12] In 1569 Silvius edited the *Epigrammata* of Janus Dousa, and through his

---

[4] Aulotte, op. cit., p. 166, n. 1.

[5] M. Aulotte very kindly informed me in January 1967 that he had so far not come across any other copy, apart from the odd volume in the Bibliothèque Nationale.

[6] Colin Clair, " Willem Silvius ", in *The Library* XIV (1959), 192-205.

[7] Ibid., p. 193 ; cf. Colin Clair, *Christopher Plantin*, London, 1960, p. 273.

[8] This information is from an anonymous article " Quelques notes sur Guillaume Silvius, Imprimeur d'Anvers " in *Bulletin du Bibliophile Belge* XVIII (1862), 122-159.

[9] Cf. *Biographie Nationale de Belgique*, 1914-20, t. 22, col. 512.

[10] Cf. *Bulletin du Bibliophile Belge*, loc. cit.

[11] Cf. article by Colin Clair in *The Library* XIV (1959), 196.

[12] Cf. *Bulletin du Bibliophile Belge*, loc. cit.

influence he became printer to the University of Leyden in June 1577. He moved there in 1579, establishing his presses at the sign of the golden angel (in der gulden enghel), the device which he had used since 1561. He died in August or September 1580. He was succeeded in his business by his son Charles, aided by his widow, but before the end of 1582 they had handed the business over to Christopher Plantin.[13]

If we turn now to the early editions of the *Vies* in Amyot's translation we find that they are basically the same but that there are a few differences. The first edition has a prefatory letter to Henri II which bears the date February 1559 and an *achevé d'imprimer* dated May of the same year. It contains also a general privilege, dated February 1553, for ten years, " pour tous les liures que ledit Vascosan imprimera cy apres, lesquels n'auront esté auparauant imprimez en nostredit Royaume : Et six ans pour ceux lesquels par la collation de plusieurs bons et diuers exemplaires, et par le labeur, diligence et industrie dudit Vascosan, et des hommes doctes, de grande literature et experience et probité et integrité auront esté remis, restituez et illustrez de notables corrections, emendations et annotations, à commencer du iour et date de la premiere impression de chacun desdits liures ". This first edition contains, too, after the *Aux lecteurs*, fourteen lines of verse entitled " inuention d'Agathius Scholasticus Poete Grec " which Silvius does not reproduce. The Antwerp edition does, however, copy the first edition in prefacing the text with Amyot's dedication to Henri II, the long *Aux lecteurs*, and the table of contents (Catalogue des Hommes Illustres Grecs et Romains) although this latter refers to each volume's contents and not those of the whole work.[14]

The first edition contains a list of " fautes et corrections ". The second edition (so-called) was started in 1563 and when it appeared in 1565 it incorporated these corrections and some others. But the Antwerp edition had already made these corrections (e.g., " Cariolanus " changed to " Coriolanus "—this was not one of the corrections listed, " Theseus donques " changed to " Aegeus donques ", " qu'ilz se sont " changed to " qui se sont ", to mention only the first two listed).[15] Amyot himself does not seem to have seen the Antwerp edition, or if he has, then he is anxious to cover up the fact that it was correct and accurate. He felt that " les fautes commises en la premiere impression, par inaduertance ou faute d'exemplaire biē correct demoureroient en la seconde impression ". In reality it *had* made use of his list of corrections and made some other necessary emendations which he had not suggested.

The spelling of the three texts is not identical, but the variations lack consistency ; if we list some examples in order (1559, 1564, 1565) we find :

[13] For further information on Silvius see P. A. Tiele, " Les premiers imprimeurs de l'université de Leide, (Les Silvius, Christophe Plantin, Les Ravelinghen.) " in *Le Bibliophile belge*, 1869, pp. 83-87 ; and Colin Clair, *Christopher Plantin*, London, 1960, passim.

[14] Volume one goes from Theseus to Marcus Cato, volume two from Philopoemen to Julius Caesar.

[15] For a discussion of the errata cf. Sturel, op. cit., p. 96.

doyūet, doiuēt, doyuent ; second, secōd, second ; pourautāt, pour-autant, pourautant.

The title of the book is the same except for minor spelling variations : " Les Vies des Hommes Illustres Grecs et Romains Comparees l'une auec l'autre par Plutarque de Chæronęe, Translatees de Grec en François ". At this point there is divergence, because in the 1559 edition Amyot's name does not appear until the second page, at the head of the prefatory letter, whereas Silvius puts on the title-page " par Iacques Amyot Abbé de Bellozane ". The Antwerp edition then has three items which are not in the other editions. The phrase " Et divisees en III. Tomes " is followed by " Ausquelles de nouueau sont adioustees les vies d'Hannibal et de Scipion l'Africain ". This is followed by " Ce vray miroir ancien d'humaine police Doibt seruir de reflexe en toute monarchie ". There are 478 ff. in my edition, but at least one page has been torn out at the end. The book lacks the end of the life of Marcus Cato and whatever else may have followed it, though there are 6 ff. blank. The title-page of volume two is similar except that between the words " Plutarque de Cheronæe " and the printer's device there is nothing except " Tome II ". For some reason the golden angel in volume one divides the motto " SCRVTA/MINI " and in volume two " SCRV/ TAMINI ". Volume two contains 514 ff. and the last page ends " Fin du Second Tome " and lists five " Faultes trouuees ". The only other point of interest concerns the lives of Hannibal and Scipio Africanus, especially the latter since it was at exactly this time that Amyot himself was composing his life of Scipio (the Greek text of which had been lost).[16] Since we have no volume three we do not know if these lives were ever published by Silvius. They are referred to again on the back of the title-page of volume one in the Extraict du Priuilege. This is worth quoting in full since it does not appear in the Bibliothèque Nationale copy : " Il a pleu au Roy nostre Sire donner Priuilege à Guillaume Silvius, son imprimeur Royal, d'imprimer *Les vies des hommes illustres Grecs et Romains, comparées l'vne auec l'autre par Plutarque de Cheronæe, translatées de Grec en François par Iacques Amyot Abbé de Bellozane*. Ausquelles ledict Silvius a de nouueau fait adiouster *Les deux vies d'Hānibal et de Scipion l'Africain* : et sont faites deffences à tous autres imprimeurs et libraires d'imprimer, vendre ou distribuer és terres et seigneuries dudict Seigneur le susdit liure iusques au temps et terme de six ans consecutifs sur grādes peines, comme plus à plein est contenu en l'original, donné à Brucelles le 2. du mois de Decembre 1562. Seigné De Perre ".

It is perhaps odd that there are no other extant copies of the Antwerp edition, unless some attempt was made to sell them in France and the copies were seized, as Vascosan's privilege threatened. Two questions remain : was the third volume ever printed, and what happened to the book in some other format mentioned in 1563 ? A possible answer to the second question is that this book refers to the *Tresor des Vies* of 1567.

PETER SHARRATT

Edinburgh

[16] Cf. Sturel, op. cit., p. 97.